Fundamentals of
Business
Analytics

Unlocking Data-Driven Insights for Successful Business

Rohith B
Kumar P

Preface

In today's fast-paced and data-driven world, businesses are increasingly turning to data analytics to make informed decisions, optimize operations, and stay competitive. The ability to harness data, uncover insights, and translate them into actionable strategies has become a critical skill for professionals across all industries. Fundamentals of Business Analytics is designed to introduce readers to the core principles and techniques of business analytics and provide a solid foundation for anyone looking to leverage data to drive business success.

The field of business analytics encompasses a variety of methods, from descriptive analytics, which helps to understand past performance, to predictive and prescriptive analytics, which enable organizations to forecast trends and make optimal decisions. This book covers the essential concepts and tools in each of these areas, making it accessible to beginners while still providing valuable insights for those with more experience in the field.

Each chapter is designed to build upon the previous one, taking the reader from basic statistical techniques to more advanced models such as machine learning and optimization. Through real-world practical examples, and hands-on exercises, readers will gain a deep understanding of how to apply analytics to solve business problems, improve decision-making, and drive value across organizations.

One of the key objectives of this book is to demystify the complexities of business analytics. In doing so, we emphasize the importance of understanding the business context before diving into data analysis. The techniques discussed throughout the book are not just theoretical concepts but are grounded in real-world applications, where data-driven decisions can make a tangible impact on an organization's success.

As you read this book, remember that business analytics is not just about crunching numbers or using sophisticated algorithms. It is about using data to tell a story, guide decisions, and create opportunities for innovation and growth. Whether you're a student just starting your journey into business analytics, a professional seeking to enhance your skills, or a decision-maker aiming to lead your organization toward more data-driven strategies, Fundamentals of Business Analytics will provide you with the knowledge and tools to navigate this exciting and ever-evolving field.

We hope this book inspires you to explore the power of business analytics and empowers you to apply these techniques to solve real-world business challenges.

Table of Contents

1. Introduction to Business Analytics

Business Analytics (BA) refers to the use of data, statistical analysis, and modeling to make informed business decisions. It involves analyzing historical data to uncover patterns, trends, and insights that can guide future actions. Business Analytics is widely applied in various industries such as marketing, finance, operations, and human resources to improve decision-making processes, optimize business performance, and gain a competitive advantage. Let us understand the basics of Data Analytics before we discuss Business Analytics.

What is Data?

Data refers to raw facts, figures, or information collected and recorded for analysis or reference. It can come in various forms—numerical, textual, visual, or even sensory information—and can be structured (organized in a specific format, like a table) or unstructured (like text, audio, or images).

In the context of business, data might include sales figures, customer information, product details, transaction histories, market trends, and more. The key aspect of data is that it's generally unprocessed, which means it does not provide immediate insights without further interpretation or analysis.

Types of Data:

1. **Structured Data**: Data that is highly organized and stored in a fixed format, often in relational databases (e.g., spreadsheets, tables). Examples: customer information, sales transactions.

2. **Unstructured Data**: Data that lacks a predefined structure. Examples: social media posts, email messages, video content, or customer feedback.

3. **Semi-structured Data**: Data that has some level of organization, but not in a tabular format. Examples: JSON, XML files.

What is Data Analysis?

Data Analysis refers to the process of inspecting, cleaning, transforming, and modeling data in order to discover useful information, draw conclusions, and support decision-making. It's a key component of data-driven decision-making and helps businesses and organizations make sense of raw data.

The data analysis process typically involves:

1. **Data Collection**: Gathering data from various sources.

2. **Data Cleaning**: Removing inaccuracies, dealing with missing values, and correcting inconsistencies.

3. **Data Transformation**: Converting data into a usable format or structure.

4. **Exploratory Data Analysis (EDA)**: Summarizing the main characteristics of the data, often using visual methods like charts and graphs.

5. **Statistical Analysis**: Applying mathematical and statistical techniques to interpret the data (e.g., regression, hypothesis testing).

6. **Modeling**: Creating models to predict future outcomes (e.g., predictive analytics, machine learning).

7. **Visualization**: Presenting findings in a visual format to facilitate understanding and communication.

Key Steps in Data Analysis:

- **Descriptive Analysis**: Describes the characteristics of a dataset (e.g., mean, median, standard deviation).

- **Diagnostic Analysis**: Identifies relationships and reasons for trends or outcomes in the data.

- **Predictive Analysis**: Uses statistical models and machine learning to predict future trends or behavior.

- **Prescriptive Analysis**: Provides recommendations for actions based on analysis (e.g., optimizing inventory levels, pricing strategies).

What is Business Data Analysis?

Business Data Analysis is the process of applying data analysis techniques specifically to business data to help organizations make informed decisions and solve business problems. It involves looking at business-related data (like sales, customer feedback, financial records) to gain insights that can drive strategy, improve operations, and achieve business goals.

Business Data Analysis typically includes:

1. **Identifying Key Business Metrics**: Metrics such as sales revenue, customer acquisition costs, profit margins, churn rates, and market share.

2. **Analyzing Trends and Patterns**: Detecting patterns in sales, customer behavior, or market trends that can help in decision-making.

3. **Optimizing Business Operations**: Using data to streamline processes, reduce costs, improve efficiency, and maximize ROI (Return on Investment).

4. **Customer Insights**: Understanding customer preferences, behaviors, and needs through data to improve marketing strategies, product offerings, and customer service.

5. **Competitive Analysis**: Comparing business performance against competitors by analyzing external data like market share, industry trends, or pricing strategies.

Example:

- A retail business analyzing customer purchasing behavior data to identify which products are most popular during certain months.

- A company analyzing financial statements to identify areas where costs can be reduced or where investments can yield higher returns.

Business Analytics is the practice of using data, statistical analysis, and quantitative methods to drive business decision-making and improve organizational performance. It involves collecting and analyzing historical data to uncover patterns, trends, and insights that can inform strategies and optimize operations. Business analytics can encompass a wide range of techniques, from basic descriptive analytics (summarizing past performance) to advanced predictive and prescriptive analytics (forecasting future outcomes and recommending actions). By leveraging business analytics, companies can make data-driven decisions that enhance customer satisfaction, streamline processes, increase profitability, and gain a competitive edge in the market.

Key Components of Business Analytics:

1. **Descriptive Analytics**: Analyzes past data to understand what happened. This is typically done through reporting and data visualization.

2. **Predictive Analytics**: Uses historical data and statistical techniques to predict future outcomes or trends. It helps businesses anticipate potential problems or opportunities.

3. **Prescriptive Analytics**: Provides recommendations on how to handle potential future situations. It focuses on decision-making based on predictions.

4. **Diagnostic Analytics**: Investigates data to understand why something happened. It often includes root cause analysis.

Example: Sales Analysis Using Business Analytics

Let's explore an example where a company wants to analyze its sales data to understand the relationship between advertising spend and sales performance, with the goal of optimizing marketing spend.

Objective: The company wants to determine if increasing the advertising budget leads to increased sales, and at what point the returns diminish.

Sample Data:

We'll look at a simplified dataset that tracks monthly sales and advertising spend for the past six months.

Month	Advertising Spend ($)	Sales Revenue ($)
Jan	10,000	100,000
Feb	12,000	120,000
Mar	15,000	145,000
Apr	18,000	150,000
May	20,000	160,000
Jun	22,000	165,000

Results of the Analysis:

- **Correlation**: The company wants to find out the correlation between advertising spend and sales. The correlation can be calculated using a statistical method such as Pearson's correlation coefficient.

In this case, we calculate the correlation coefficient, which comes out to approximately **0.98**, indicating a very strong positive relationship between advertising spend and sales. This suggests that as advertising spend increases, sales tend to increase as well.

- **Regression Analysis**: Next, a linear regression model can be used to predict sales based on advertising spend. The linear regression equation might look something like this:

$$\text{Sales} = 50,000 + 5 \times (\text{Advertising Spend})$$

This means that for every additional dollar spent on advertising, sales increase by $5. The intercept of $50,000 represents the baseline sales when advertising spend is $0 (i.e., sales are still $50,000 even without any advertising).

Interpretation of Results:

- **Positive Correlation**: The strong positive correlation (0.98) confirms that more advertising spend leads to higher sales. This is expected in most cases where marketing efforts directly influence sales.

- **Regression Analysis**: From the regression model, we see that the company's sales are positively influenced by advertising. However, it is important to note that the relationship might not continue to hold indefinitely. At some point, the returns on additional advertising spend may diminish, which would require a more advanced model like nonlinear regression or an analysis of diminishing returns.

Predictions Based on the Model:

Using the regression equation, we can predict the sales for a given advertising spend. For example, if the company plans to spend $25,000 on advertising next month, the predicted sales would be:

$$\text{Sales} = 50,000 + 5 \times 25,000 = 50,000 + 125,000 = 175,000$$

So, the company could expect to generate $175,000 in sales if it spends $25,000 on advertising.

Conclusion:

From the analysis, we can conclude that the company's sales have a strong positive relationship with its advertising spend, and based on the regression model, the company can predict sales for various levels of advertising spend. However, as the company increases its advertising budget, it should consider the potential for diminishing returns, which could be modeled more accurately with a different approach. This information can help guide future decisions on optimal advertising spend to maximize sales without overspending.

This kind of analysis allows businesses to make data-driven decisions to optimize their marketing strategies and improve profitability.

1.1 Definition and Scope of Business Analytics

Business Analytics (BA) refers to the process of collecting, processing, analyzing, and interpreting large sets of data to help organizations make more informed decisions and improve business outcomes. It involves applying statistical methods, algorithms, and tools to understand business performance, identify trends, make predictions, and ultimately guide decision-making processes. BA is crucial in today's data-driven business environment, where data is a valuable asset for organizations seeking competitive advantages.

Business Analytics encompasses various types of analysis, each with its own objective, but all aimed at providing actionable insights for decision-makers.

Types of Business Analytics

1. **Descriptive Analytics**:

   o **Objective**: To describe what has happened in the past.

   o **Example**: Analyzing past sales data to understand trends or summarize financial performance.

2. **Diagnostic Analytics**:

   o **Objective**: To determine why something happened.

   o **Example**: Investigating why sales dropped in a particular quarter, identifying factors such as seasonality or market conditions.

3. **Predictive Analytics**:

   o **Objective**: To predict what is likely to happen in the future.

   o **Example**: Using historical sales data to forecast future demand or sales figures.

4. **Prescriptive Analytics**:

   o **Objective**: To recommend actions for the future.

   o **Example**: Recommending changes to the supply chain process based on predictive analysis to reduce costs or improve service delivery.

Scope of Business Analytics

The scope of Business Analytics is vast and covers multiple aspects of business functions, including:

1. **Marketing Analytics**:

- o Optimizing marketing strategies by analyzing customer behavior, engagement metrics, and campaign effectiveness.
- o Example: Identifying the most profitable customer segments or channels.

2. **Financial Analytics**:
   - o Monitoring financial performance, forecasting revenues and expenditures, and detecting anomalies in financial records.
   - o Example: Predicting cash flows or identifying fraudulent transactions.

3. **Operational Analytics**:
   - o Improving efficiency and streamlining business processes, such as inventory management or production scheduling.
   - o Example: Reducing supply chain inefficiencies or optimizing staffing schedules.

4. **Customer Analytics**:
   - o Analyzing customer data to improve customer satisfaction and loyalty.
   - o Example: Segmenting customers based on purchasing behavior and tailoring marketing strategies.

5. **Human Resource Analytics**:
   - o Analyzing employee data for better talent management, employee engagement, and retention.
   - o Example: Identifying predictors of employee turnover and devising retention strategies.

Example:

1. Analyzing Customer Sales Data (Descriptive Analytics)

Let's consider a retail company that wants to understand how its sales performance varies across different store locations. The company collects data from its five store locations over the last 6 months and aims to identify which stores are performing the best.

Sample Data (Sales by Store Location)

Month	Store A Sales ($)	Store B Sales ($)	Store C Sales ($)	Store D Sales ($)	Store E Sales ($)
Jan	50,000	60,000	55,000	45,000	40,000
Feb	55,000	62,000	58,000	47,000	42,000
Mar	53,000	64,000	57,000	46,000	41,000
Apr	52,000	61,000	56,000	45,000	43,000
May	58,000	65,000	59,000	48,000	44,000
Jun	60,000	68,000	60,000	49,000	45,000

Results of the Analysis:

To better understand the sales performance, we can calculate the following:

1. **Total Sales per Store** (Sum of sales across all months)
2. **Average Sales per Store** (Average sales per month for each store)
3. **Sales Ranking** (Rank the stores based on total or average sales)

Calculations:

Store	Total Sales ($)	Average Sales ($)	Sales Rank
Store A	328,000	54,667	3
Store B	380,000	63,333	1
Store C	349,000	58,167	2
Store D	270,000	45,000	5
Store E	255,000	42,500	6

Explanation of Results:

- **Store B** has the highest total sales ($380,000), followed by **Store C** with $349,000 in sales. These two stores also have the highest average sales per month, indicating consistent strong performance.

- **Store A** ranks third, with total sales of $328,000, averaging $54,667 per month, which is slightly lower than Store B and Store C but still shows healthy sales performance.

- **Store D** and **Store E** have lower sales figures, with Store D ranking 5th and Store E ranking 6th. These stores have the lowest average sales, which could be due to factors such as location, customer demographics, or marketing efforts.

Insights and Business Decisions:

- **Store B**: As the top performer, this store might be a model for others. It could be valuable to investigate what factors contribute to its success (e.g., location, promotions, product assortment, customer service).

- **Store D and Store E**: These stores are underperforming. The company might consider conducting a diagnostic analysis to understand the root causes (e.g., poor customer traffic, competition, store management). Additionally, the company might explore targeted marketing campaigns or operational improvements in these locations to boost sales.

- **Overall Performance**: The company can use this data to allocate resources more effectively, focusing marketing efforts or inventory management on the better-performing stores while addressing underperformance in others.

2. Diagnostic Analytics: Understanding Why Something Happened

Objective: Diagnostic analytics investigates why certain events or outcomes happened. It uses historical data to identify factors and causes that influenced the observed results.

Example Scenario: Sales Decline in Store D

We saw earlier that **Store D** had the lowest sales among the five locations. Diagnostic analytics can help us investigate the cause of the sales decline in Store D compared to other stores.

Sample Data (Customer Foot Traffic vs. Sales)

Month	Store D Sales ($)	Store D Foot Traffic	Store B Sales ($)	Store B Foot Traffic
Jan	45,000	5,000	60,000	8,000
Feb	47,000	5,200	62,000	8,200
Mar	46,000	5,100	64,000	8,500
Apr	45,000	5,000	61,000	8,300
May	48,000	5,300	65,000	8,600

| Jun | 49,000 | 5,400 | 68,000 | 8,800 |

Calculation: Sales per Customer (Sales / Foot Traffic)

Month	Store D Sales ($)	Store D Foot Traffic	Sales per Customer (Store D)	Store B Sales ($)	Store B Foot Traffic	Sales per Customer (Store B)
Jan	45,000	5,000	9	60,000	8,000	7.5
Feb	47,000	5,200	9.04	62,000	8,200	7.56
Mar	46,000	5,100	9.02	64,000	8,500	7.53
Apr	45,000	5,000	9	61,000	8,300	7.35
May	48,000	5,300	9.05	65,000	8,600	7.56
Jun	49,000	5,400	9.07	68,000	8,800	7.73

Diagnostic Analysis:

- **Sales per Customer**: For **Store D**, the "Sales per Customer" is consistently higher than **Store B**, which indicates that each customer in Store D is spending more on average than those in Store B.

- **Foot Traffic**: However, Store D's **foot traffic** is significantly lower than Store B's. This is likely the primary reason for the sales decline—fewer customers are visiting Store D, which is causing the total sales to be lower despite each customer spending more.

Observation:

Diagnostic analytics suggests that the key reason behind Store D's sales decline is lower foot traffic, not poor sales per customer. This indicates that improving customer attraction (through promotions, location optimization, etc.) could be a more effective strategy than focusing on individual customer sales.

3. Predictive Analytics: Predicting Future Outcomes

Objective: Predictive analytics uses historical data and statistical models to forecast future trends or outcomes. It is typically used to anticipate future sales, customer behavior, or other key metrics.

Example Scenario: Forecasting Sales for Store A

Using the data from the previous months, we will now apply a simple linear regression model to predict sales for **Store A** in the next month (July).

Sample Data (Sales in Store A for the Past 6 Months)

Month	Store A Sales ($)
Jan	50,000
Feb	55,000
Mar	53,000
Apr	52,000
May	58,000
Jun	60,000

Calculation: Linear Regression Model

We'll fit a simple linear regression model:

$$\text{Sales} = a + b \times (\text{Month})$$

Where:

- a is the intercept.
- b is the slope (rate of change).

Using statistical software or a tool like Excel, we can calculate the regression coefficients. Let's assume the regression equation is:

$$\text{Sales} = 50,000 + 2,000 \times (\text{Month})$$

This indicates that sales increase by $2,000 per month.

Prediction for July (Month 7):

$$\text{Sales for July} = 50,000 + 2,000 \times 7 = 50,000 + 14,000 = 64,000$$

Results:

Month	Store A Sales ($)	Predicted Sales for July ($)
Jan	50,000	

Feb	55,000	
Mar	53,000	
Apr	52,000	
May	58,000	
Jun	60,000	
July		**64,000**

Observation:

Using the predictive model, we can forecast that **Store A**'s sales in July will be approximately **$64,000**. This helps the company prepare for future revenue and plan its inventory and marketing strategies accordingly. Predictive analytics provides businesses with foresight, which allows them to make proactive decisions.

4. Prescriptive Analytics: Recommending the Best Course of Action

Objective: Prescriptive analytics provides actionable recommendations based on the insights generated from predictive and descriptive analytics. It helps businesses decide the best course of action to achieve desired outcomes.

Example Scenario: Optimizing Advertising Spend

Based on the past data, a company wants to determine how much to spend on advertising to maximize sales. The company has a budget of $30,000 for advertising and wants to optimize its spend for maximum returns.

Sample Data (Advertising Spend vs. Sales)

Month	Advertising Spend ($)	Sales ($)
Jan	10,000	100,000
Feb	12,000	120,000
Mar	15,000	145,000
Apr	18,000	150,000
May	20,000	160,000
Jun	22,000	165,000

Calculation: Linear Regression for Sales vs. Advertising Spend

We apply a linear regression to model sales as a function of advertising spend. Assume the regression equation we derive is:

$$\text{Sales} = 50,000 + 5 \times (\text{Advertising Spend})$$

So, for every $1 spent on advertising, sales increase by $5.

Predicting Sales for $30,000 Advertising Spend:

$$\text{Sales} = 50,000 + 5 \times 30,000 = 50,000 + 150,000 = 200,000$$

Results:

Advertising Spend ($)	Predicted Sales ($)
10,000	100,000
12,000	110,000
15,000	125,000
18,000	140,000
20,000	150,000
22,000	160,000
30,000	**200,000**

Observation:

Prescriptive analytics suggests that if the company spends $30,000 on advertising, it can expect to generate $200,000 in sales. This gives the company clear guidance on how much to spend to maximize its revenue, based on the predictive model. Additionally, the company can consider factors like diminishing returns if it goes beyond a certain threshold, which might require more advanced modeling (such as nonlinear regression).

Summary of Analytics Types:

1. **Descriptive Analytics** helped to allocate resources more effectively, focusing marketing efforts or inventory management on the better-performing stores while addressing underperformance in others.

2. **Diagnostic Analytics** helped identify that **Store D's** sales decline is due to lower foot traffic.

3. **Predictive Analytics** forecasted that **Store A's** sales in July will be around **$64,000**, based on historical trends.

4. **Prescriptive Analytics** recommended that spending **$30,000** on advertising could increase sales to **$200,000**, helping the company optimize its marketing budget.

These different types of analytics work together to provide a comprehensive view of the business, from understanding past performance to predicting future trends and recommending optimal actions.

Examples on Scope of Business Analytics

Let's extend the previous examples by exploring four more key areas where analytics is widely applied in business: **Marketing Analytics, Financial Analytics, Operational Analytics**, and **Human Resource Analytics**. Each of these focuses on different aspects of business performance, providing actionable insights to optimize decisions and strategies.

1. Marketing Analytics: Analyzing Campaign Effectiveness

Objective: Marketing analytics helps measure and optimize marketing campaigns by analyzing customer behavior, engagement metrics, and the return on investment (ROI).

Example Scenario: Evaluating the Effectiveness of a Marketing Campaign

A company recently ran a marketing campaign targeting its customer base to boost sales. They want to analyze the effectiveness of the campaign by examining the relationship between campaign spending and sales performance.

Sample Data (Marketing Campaign Spend vs. Sales)

Month	Marketing Spend ($)	Sales ($)	New Customers Acquired
Jan	5,000	50,000	200
Feb	6,000	55,000	250
Mar	8,000	70,000	300
Apr	7,500	65,000	270
May	9,000	75,000	350
Jun	10,000	80,000	400

Calculation: Customer Acquisition Cost (CAC)

The **Customer Acquisition Cost (CAC)** is calculated by dividing the marketing spend by the number of new customers acquired each month.

Month	Marketing Spend ($)	New Customers	CAC ($) = Marketing Spend / New Customers
Jan	5,000	200	25
Feb	6,000	250	24
Mar	8,000	300	26.67
Apr	7,500	270	27.78
May	9,000	350	25.71
Jun	10,000	400	25

Analysis:

- **Cost Efficiency**: The CAC fluctuates between $24 and $27.78, with **May** being the most cost-effective month in terms of acquiring new customers.

- **Sales Growth**: As marketing spend increases, sales also increase, suggesting that the campaign is effective in driving sales. However, the relationship between marketing spend and new customers is more consistent in May and June, indicating diminishing returns after a certain point.

Observation:

Marketing analytics suggests that while increasing marketing spend helps drive sales and acquire new customers, there is an optimal point at which additional spending yields diminishing returns. The company might focus on maintaining an efficient CAC around $25–26 while maximizing returns from future campaigns.

2. Financial Analytics: Analyzing Profitability

Objective: Financial analytics focuses on measuring and optimizing financial performance by analyzing financial statements, profitability, and cost structures.

Example Scenario: Analyzing Profit Margins Across Different Products

A company sells three different products and wants to analyze the profitability of each product to decide which one to focus on for future growth.

Sample Data (Sales, Costs, and Profit for Three Products)

Product	Sales ($)	Cost of Goods Sold (COGS) ($)	Gross Profit ($)	Gross Profit Margin (%)
Product A	100,000	60,000	40,000	40%
Product B	150,000	90,000	60,000	40%
Product C	80,000	30,000	50,000	62.50%

Calculation: Gross Profit Margin (%)

The **Gross Profit Margin** is calculated as:

$$\text{Gross Profit Margin} = \frac{\text{Gross Profit}}{\text{Sales}} \times 100$$

Product	Sales ($)	Cost of Goods Sold (COGS) ($)	Gross Profit ($)	Gross Profit Margin (%)
Product A	100,000	60,000	40,000	40%
Product B	150,000	90,000	60,000	40%
Product C	80,000	30,000	50,000	62.50%

Analysis:

- **Gross Profit Margin**: **Product C** has the highest gross profit margin (62.5%), meaning it is the most profitable product on a per-dollar basis. In contrast, both **Product A** and **Product B** have a gross profit margin of 40%, indicating they are less profitable than Product C.

- **Sales Volume**: **Product B** has the highest sales, but despite this, it has the same gross profit margin as Product A, which may suggest that **Product B** has higher variable costs or less efficient production processes.

Observation:

From a financial analytics perspective, **Product C** is the most profitable in terms of gross margin. If the company aims to improve overall profitability, it could focus more on promoting **Product C**, possibly expanding its production or marketing efforts. **Product B's** high sales volume is important, but its margin is relatively lower, so the company should consider ways to reduce costs or increase prices to improve profitability.

3. Operational Analytics: Optimizing Inventory Management

Objective: Operational analytics focuses on optimizing business operations by analyzing workflows, resource utilization, inventory management, and supply chain efficiency.

Example Scenario: Inventory and Stockouts Analysis

A company wants to analyze its inventory management to minimize stockouts (when items are unavailable for sale). They examine inventory levels and sales data to optimize their inventory replenishment process.

Sample Data (Inventory, Sales, and Stockouts)

Month	Product A Inventory (units)	Product A Sales (units)	Stockouts (units)	Product B Inventory (units)	Product B Sales (units)	Stockouts (units)
Jan	500	400	0	300	350	50
Feb	450	420	30	280	300	20
Mar	480	460	20	250	300	30
Apr	500	450	0	270	290	30
May	520	470	10	260	280	40
Jun	500	480	20	240	270	30

Analysis:

- **Stockout Trends**: **Product A** has fewer stockouts than **Product B**, but both products experience stockouts every month. In **February**, **Product B** faces a particularly high stockout rate, with 50 units unavailable.

- **Sales vs. Inventory**: **Product A** consistently sells close to its available inventory, while **Product B** has higher sales than its inventory in January and February, leading to stockouts.

Observation:

The operational analytics suggests that the company should consider adjusting inventory levels based on sales trends, especially for **Product B**, which experiences frequent stockouts. Implementing an inventory optimization model (such as **Just-in-Time (JIT)**) could help minimize stockouts and reduce excess inventory for both products, optimizing operational efficiency and reducing costs associated with overstocking.

4. Human Resource Analytics: Employee Turnover Analysis

Objective: Human resource analytics helps optimize talent management, employee retention, and workforce planning by analyzing employee data and turnover trends.

Example Scenario: Analyzing Employee Turnover

The company wants to understand the factors contributing to employee turnover and how to reduce it. They analyze employee data over the past year to identify trends in voluntary resignations.

Sample Data (Employee Turnover, Age, and Tenure)

Month	Employees Left	Average Age (Years)	Average Tenure (Years)	Department
Jan	5	35	3	Sales
Feb	3	38	4	Marketing
Mar	6	32	2	IT
Apr	4	36	3.5	Operations
May	7	30	1.5	Sales
Jun	5	37	4	HR

Calculation: Turnover Rate (Turnover / Total Employees)

Month	Employees Left	Total Employees	Turnover Rate (%) = Employees Left / Total Employees * 100
Jan	5	50	10%
Feb	3	50	6%
Mar	6	55	10.91%
Apr	4	55	7.27%
May	7	55	12.73%
Jun	5	50	10%

Analysis:

- **Turnover Trends**: **Sales** department experiences the highest turnover rates, especially in **May** (12.73%), despite a relatively average age (30 years) and tenure (1.5 years). The **IT** department has a higher turnover rate in **March** (10.91%) than other months, which could indicate challenges with employee retention in tech roles.

- **Employee Profile**: Younger employees with less tenure seem to leave more frequently, suggesting potential issues related to employee engagement or career growth opportunities for newer hires.

Observation:

Human resource analytics indicates that the **Sales** department is facing higher turnover rates and might need improvements in employee engagement, training, or compensation packages. Furthermore, addressing retention strategies for younger employees with shorter tenures could help reduce turnover and improve organizational stability. A deeper analysis of exit interviews and employee satisfaction surveys could provide more insights into specific reasons behind turnover.

Summary of Analytics Types:

1. **Marketing Analytics** helped identify the **Customer Acquisition Cost (CAC)** and suggested efficient campaign management strategies.

2. **Financial Analytics** revealed that **Product C** offers the highest gross profit margin, guiding the company toward more profitable product strategies.

3. **Operational Analytics** highlighted inventory issues and suggested optimizing inventory management to minimize stockouts.

4. **Human Resource Analytics** uncovered high turnover rates in the **Sales** department and provided insights on improving employee retention strategies.

Each of these analytics areas provides valuable insights that help businesses improve performance, optimize strategies, and make data-driven decisions across different functional domains.

1.2 Descriptive Analytics

Descriptive Analytics is the process of summarizing and interpreting historical data to understand what has happened in the past. In business, it helps companies gain insights into their operations, customers, and overall performance by analyzing data that has already been collected.

Instead of making predictions (like predictive analytics) or giving recommendations (like prescriptive analytics), **descriptive analytics** simply focuses on understanding the data and highlighting trends, patterns, and key metrics from the past.

Key Concepts of Descriptive Analytics in Business

1. **Summarizing Data**: Descriptive analytics summarizes data into meaningful insights, often using key metrics such as averages, totals, trends, and percentages. This summary helps businesses understand past performance.

2. **Trend Analysis**: It helps identify trends over time (e.g., sales increase or decrease, customer behavior changes, or seasonal patterns).

3. **Data Visualization**: Descriptive analytics often uses charts, graphs, and dashboards to make the insights more accessible and easier to interpret for decision-makers.

4. **Performance Metrics**: Descriptive analytics involves calculating key business metrics such as:

   o **Revenue**: Total income from sales.

   o **Profit**: Revenue minus costs.

   o **Customer Acquisition**: The number of new customers gained.

   o **Sales Performance**: How much product is sold in a given period.

   o **Employee Performance**: Productivity or efficiency metrics.

5. **Historical Data Analysis**: By analyzing past data, businesses can understand historical performance, spot patterns, and generate insights that provide a solid foundation for further analysis and decision-making.

Example of Descriptive Analytics in Business

Let's consider a **retail store** that wants to analyze its **monthly sales data** to understand performance over the past six months.

Sample Business Data Table (Sales Data)

Month	Sales ($)
January	15,000
February	18,000
March	22,000
April	20,000
May	25,000
June	30,000

Descriptive Analytics Insights

Descriptive analytics in this scenario will help the business understand the following key points:

1. **Total Sales**: The total revenue generated over the last six months.

2. **Average Sales**: The average monthly sales over the period.

3. **Sales Trend**: How sales have changed month-to-month.

4. **Sales Growth**: How sales have grown or shrunk compared to previous months.

5. **Month with Highest/Lowest Sales**: Identifying which month had the best and worst performance.

Output and Results Based on Descriptive Analytics

Month	Sales ($)	Cumulative Sales ($)	Growth (%)	Remarks
January	15,000	15,000	-	Starting point
February	18,000	33,000	20%	Sales increased by 20%
March	22,000	55,000	22.20%	Sales increased by 22.2%
April	20,000	75,000	-9.10%	Sales decreased by 9.1%
May	25,000	100,000	25%	Sales increased by 25%
June	30,000	130,000	20%	Sales increased by 20%
Total	**130,000**	-	-	Total sales for the 6 months

Average	21,667	-	-	Average sales per month

Explanation and Interpretation of Results

1. **Total Sales**: Over the six-month period, the company has generated **$130,000** in sales. This is the total revenue from all the months combined. Descriptive analytics helps provide a snapshot of total business performance.

2. **Average Sales**: The average sales per month is **$21,667**. This is calculated by dividing the total sales by the number of months. It provides an overall sense of how well the company is performing month-to-month.

3. **Sales Growth**: By comparing month-to-month sales, we can identify growth trends:

    o   February to March saw a **22.2% increase**.

    o   April, however, saw a **9.1% decline** in sales, which could prompt further investigation to understand why sales dropped during this month.

    o   The most significant growth occurred between April and May, with a **25% increase**.

    o   Overall, the sales growth is positive, and this trend continued into June with a **20% increase**.

4. **Cumulative Sales**: The cumulative sales column shows how the total sales accumulate over time, reaching **$130,000** by June. This helps track progress toward business goals.

5. **Month with the Highest Sales**: The month with the highest sales is **June**, with $30,000 in sales. This insight can prompt the business to investigate what drove the success during that month, such as promotions, seasonal demand, or successful marketing efforts.

6. **Month with the Lowest Sales**: **January** had the lowest sales, with $15,000. This is expected for many businesses as sales in January can be slower after the holiday season. However, understanding this dip helps businesses plan better for similar seasonal drops.

Insights from Descriptive Analytics:

- **Trend Identification**: The business can see that overall, sales are trending upward, with consistent growth from January to June. This trend is positive and suggests the business is improving its performance.

- **Performance Tracking**: Descriptive analytics allows businesses to track performance against past periods. In this case, the business had periods of growth (February-March, May-June), but also saw a dip in April. By understanding these fluctuations, the business can identify factors that contributed to sales drops or surges.

- **Decision Support**: The business might use these insights to plan for future months. For example, if they see that sales tend to dip in April, they might want to prepare with promotions or special events to boost sales during that time.

- **Strategic Planning**: Knowing that **May** and **June** had strong sales, the business could plan additional marketing efforts for those months in the coming year to capture more sales during the peak period.

Conclusion

Descriptive Analytics provides businesses with essential insights into **what has happened** in the past. It helps summarize historical performance, identify trends, and understand key metrics that form the basis for making informed decisions.

In this example, the **retail store** can use descriptive analytics to:

- Understand overall sales performance over the last six months.

- Identify months with the highest and lowest sales.

- Calculate average monthly sales, providing a benchmark for future performance.

- Analyze growth trends to inform future strategies and planning.

By leveraging descriptive analytics, businesses can optimize their operations, improve decision-making, and lay the groundwork for more advanced predictive and prescriptive analytics.

1.3 Predictive Analytics

Predictive Analytics in Business involves the use of historical data and statistical techniques to forecast future outcomes. By analyzing past trends and patterns, businesses can make informed decisions, optimize processes, and plan for the future. Predictive analytics goes beyond just understanding past performance; it empowers businesses to anticipate future needs, risks, and opportunities.

Key Concepts of Predictive Analytics in Business

1. **Data-Driven Decisions**: Predictive analytics uses data from various sources such as sales history, customer behavior, market trends, and operational performance. It helps businesses understand what is likely to happen next, based on patterns from the past.

2. **Goal-Oriented Predictions**: Businesses apply predictive analytics to a wide range of goals, such as:

   o **Sales Forecasting**: Predicting future sales based on past trends.

   o **Customer Retention**: Identifying customers who are likely to churn.

   o **Inventory Management**: Estimating demand for products to avoid overstocking or stockouts.

   o **Risk Assessment**: Predicting potential risks like fraud, default, or equipment failure.

3. **Modeling Techniques**: While specific formulas are often involved in the mathematical side of predictive analytics, the general process involves:

   o **Data Collection and Cleaning**: Gathering historical data and ensuring it is accurate and usable.

   o **Pattern Recognition**: Identifying trends or relationships in the data that can be used to forecast future events.

   o **Model Application**: Using statistical or machine learning models to generate predictions.

   o **Testing and Refining**: Comparing predictions with actual outcomes to improve the model's accuracy.

4. **Real-World Benefits**:

   o Improved decision-making.

   o Efficient resource allocation.

   o Better customer insights and personalized marketing.

   o Risk mitigation by forecasting potential challenges.

Example of Predictive Analytics in Business

Let's imagine a retail store that uses predictive analytics to forecast **future sales** based on past **monthly advertising spend**.

Sample Business Data Table

Month	Advertising Spend ($)	Sales ($)
January	5,000	20,000
February	6,000	22,000
March	7,000	25,000
April	8,000	28,000
May	9,000	30,000
June	10,000	32,000

The business wants to predict **sales** for **July** based on the **advertising spend** in June, using a predictive model.

Output of Predictive Model

Assume the predictive model (using past data) identifies a strong correlation between **advertising spend** and **sales**. Based on this, the model predicts that sales will increase in a consistent way as advertising spend increases.

Using this pattern, the model generates the following **predicted sales** for the next month (July):

Month	Advertising Spend ($)	Actual Sales ($)	Predicted Sales ($)
January	5,000	20,000	20,000
February	6,000	22,000	22,000
March	7,000	25,000	25,000
April	8,000	28,000	28,000
May	9,000	30,000	30,000
June	10,000	32,000	32,000

Month	Advertising Spend ($)	Actual Sales ($)	Predicted Sales ($)
July	11,000	-	34,000

Explanation and Interpretation of Results:

1. **Predicted Sales for July**:

   o   The predictive model forecasts that if the company increases its advertising spend to $11,000 in July, the sales will likely reach **$34,000**. This prediction is based on the trend observed from the historical data that as advertising spend increases, sales tend to grow as well.

2. **Accuracy of Predictions**:

   o   The model has successfully predicted the sales for each month (January to June), aligning the predicted sales with the actual sales. This suggests that the predictive model is likely accurate for the current trend.

3. **Predicting Future Trends**:

   o   By forecasting future sales, businesses can better plan for things like inventory, staffing, and cash flow management. For example, if the business expects to make $34,000 in sales in July, it can prepare by ensuring it has enough stock and can manage customer service resources.

4. **Improved Decision-Making**:

   o   The prediction allows the business to allocate resources more effectively. If the business knows that higher advertising spend correlates with higher sales, it can decide whether to invest more in advertising to boost sales further or use the prediction to optimize other areas of operation, like promotions or product placement.

5. **Identifying Opportunities and Risks**:

   o   The model also helps to identify risks or missed opportunities. If the company has been spending relatively little on advertising compared to competitors, they might realize they could spend more on marketing to boost their sales. Alternatively, if they have been overspending with little return, they may need to adjust their advertising strategies.

Conclusion

In this business example, **predictive analytics** is used to predict future sales based on historical patterns of **advertising spend**. The predicted sales for July ($34,000) were calculated by identifying a consistent relationship between the amount spent on advertising and the resulting sales.

Interpretation: This information empowers the business to make smarter decisions about future investments in advertising, sales strategies, and inventory planning. Predictive analytics allows the company to proactively prepare for the future, ensuring they can meet demand and optimize resources accordingly.

Limitations and Considerations:

- The model assumes that the relationship between advertising spend and sales will remain constant. In reality, other factors like market conditions, customer preferences, or seasonal variations may also influence sales.

- To improve accuracy, the model can incorporate more variables, such as promotional activities, customer demographics, or market trends.

1.4 Prescriptive Analytics

Prescriptive Analytics goes beyond **descriptive** (what happened) and **predictive** (what is likely to happen) analytics by recommending actions that businesses should take to achieve specific goals. Essentially, it provides advice on **what to do** in order to improve business outcomes, optimize decisions, and solve problems.

While predictive analytics forecasts future trends, prescriptive analytics suggests the best course of action based on those predictions. It uses algorithms, simulations, optimization, and other techniques to generate recommendations that guide business decision-making.

Key Concepts of Prescriptive Analytics in Business

1. **Recommendation Systems**: Prescriptive analytics recommends actions based on the available data. For instance, if predictive analytics forecasts that sales will increase in the next quarter, prescriptive analytics may recommend increasing inventory or adjusting the marketing strategy to capture this demand.

2. **Optimization**: Prescriptive analytics often uses optimization models to determine the best solution from a set of possible choices. For example, it can help a company decide the most efficient way to allocate resources (such as budget or labor) to maximize profits or customer satisfaction.

3. **Simulation and Scenarios**: Prescriptive analytics uses simulation techniques to explore different scenarios. For example, a business might want to understand how increasing advertising spend will impact sales, and the system will simulate multiple scenarios and recommend the optimal amount to spend.

4. **Decision Support**: It provides decision-makers with actionable insights, considering various constraints (such as budget, time, and resources) and helping them make the most effective choices.

5. **Automation**: Prescriptive analytics can automate decision-making processes, suggesting actions in real-time based on ongoing data.

Example of Prescriptive Analytics in Business

Let's imagine a **retail store** that wants to optimize its **advertising spend** to achieve **maximum sales**. Based on historical data, the business has some insights into how much they typically spend on advertising and the resulting sales, but now they want to know **how much they should spend** to **achieve a target sales goal**.

Sample Business Data Table

Month	Advertising Spend ($)	Sales ($)
January	5,000	20,000
February	6,000	22,000
March	7,000	25,000
April	8,000	28,000
May	9,000	30,000
June	10,000	32,000

Prescriptive Analytics Goal

The business wants to achieve **$40,000 in sales** by **adjusting its advertising spend**. The goal is to determine the optimal advertising spend that would help the company reach that target.

Prescriptive Analytics Approach

Using prescriptive analytics, we can simulate several **scenarios** and suggest the best advertising spend needed to reach the target sales. The model might take into account various factors, including the efficiency of advertising spend at different levels, diminishing returns, and potential market conditions.

Prescriptive Recommendation

After running the analysis and optimization, the model might recommend that the company should increase its advertising spend to **$12,000** in order to achieve **$40,000 in sales**.

Predicted Table with Prescriptive Analytics Recommendations

Month	Advertising Spend ($)	Actual Sales ($)	Predicted Sales ($)	Prescriptive Recommendation (for $40,000 Sales)
January	5,000	20,000	20,000	-
February	6,000	22,000	22,000	-
March	7,000	25,000	25,000	-
April	8,000	28,000	28,000	-
May	9,000	30,000	30,000	-

Month	Advertising Spend ($)	Actual Sales ($)	Predicted Sales ($)	Prescriptive Recommendation (for $40,000 Sales)
June	10,000	32,000	32,000	-
Target	-	-	-	**$12,000**

Explanation and Interpretation of Results:

1. **Prescriptive Recommendation**: The business has a **target sales goal** of **$40,000**. Based on historical data, the prescriptive analytics model has suggested that an advertising spend of **$12,000** would likely achieve this target, optimizing the sales outcome. This recommendation is based on patterns observed from past months, where each incremental increase in advertising spend resulted in an increase in sales.

2. **Scenario Analysis**: The model considers different possible outcomes by running simulations, factoring in diminishing returns (for example, past data might show that increasing spend by $1,000 does not always result in an equal increase in sales). After evaluating all these variables, it determines the optimal budget.

3. **Actionable Insights**: By recommending a specific advertising budget, prescriptive analytics helps the business make an informed decision. Rather than simply predicting that sales will increase, it directly advises on the amount of investment required to meet the sales goal.

4. **Optimization Impact**: Prescriptive analytics is helping the business optimize its resources. Instead of guessing how much to spend or relying solely on trial and error, the store can now allocate **$12,000** in advertising with a higher confidence that it will lead to **$40,000 in sales**, optimizing the return on investment.

5. **Cost and Benefit Consideration**: This recommendation helps the business weigh the cost of advertising against the potential revenue boost. It also allows for more effective budgeting and planning by aligning marketing spend with sales goals.

Conclusion

In this case, **prescriptive analytics** has helped the business understand the optimal **advertising spend** needed to achieve a specific sales target of **$40,000**. The recommendation is not just a prediction, but a concrete action plan, providing the business with clear guidance on how to reach its goal.

Interpreting the Results:

- **Strategic Planning**: The recommendation supports decision-making by offering actionable insights, which the business can use to strategically allocate its budget and resources.

- **Optimization of Resources**: By using prescriptive analytics, the business avoids overspending or under-investing in advertising, optimizing its expenditure for maximum impact on sales.

- **Real-World Application**: This approach is widely applicable in marketing, operations, inventory management, and other business areas, enabling companies to make more data-driven and efficient decisions.

Prescriptive analytics helps businesses turn data into meaningful actions, ensuring that resources are used effectively to achieve desired outcomes.

1.5 Diagnostic Analytics

Diagnostic Analytics is the process of investigating and analyzing historical data to understand the reasons behind past outcomes. While descriptive analytics focuses on summarizing what has happened, and predictive analytics forecasts what is likely to happen, **diagnostic analytics** delves deeper into why something happened. It helps businesses identify the underlying causes of trends, problems, or anomalies.

Key Concepts of Diagnostic Analytics in Business

1. **Root Cause Analysis**: The core objective of diagnostic analytics is to identify the root causes behind certain outcomes or patterns. For example, if sales dropped, diagnostic analytics will help determine whether the cause is due to external factors like economic downturns or internal factors like marketing issues or product quality.

2. **Comparative Analysis**: It often involves comparing different variables to identify correlations. For example, diagnostic analytics might compare advertising spend with sales performance to determine if the marketing efforts were effective.

3. **Trend Analysis and Pattern Recognition**: It builds on the trends identified by descriptive analytics and investigates deeper to understand the factors driving these trends. This includes considering multiple variables and examining how they interact.

4. **Data Correlation**: Diagnostic analytics looks for relationships between variables. For instance, a business might explore the correlation between customer satisfaction scores and retention rates to determine whether satisfaction impacts long-term loyalty.

5. **Performance Evaluation**: It can be used to assess performance across different areas of the business, from sales and marketing to customer service and operations. If a department is underperforming, diagnostic analytics helps figure out why.

Example of Diagnostic Analytics in Business

Let's consider a **retail store** that has noticed a **decline in sales** over the past few months. The store wants to investigate **why** sales are declining, and diagnostic analytics can help identify the potential causes.

Sample Business Data Table (Sales and Advertising Spend)

Month	Sales ($)	Advertising Spend ($)	Customer Satisfaction Score (1-10)
January	30,000	5,000	8
February	28,000	5,500	7.5
March	27,000	6,000	7
April	25,000	7,000	6.5
May	24,000	7,500	6
June	23,000	8,000	5.5

Diagnostic Analytics Approach

The business will apply diagnostic analytics to determine the **root causes** of the sales decline. The analysis will focus on:

- The relationship between **advertising spend** and **sales**.
- The correlation between **customer satisfaction** and **sales**.

Output and Results Based on Diagnostic Analytics

Month	Sales ($)	Advertising Spend ($)	Customer Satisfaction Score (1-10)	Observations/Insights
January	30,000	5,000	8	High satisfaction and moderate advertising spend
February	28,000	5,500	7.5	Slight drop in sales, satisfaction decrease
March	27,000	6,000	7	Small decline in satisfaction, slightly higher advertising spend
April	25,000	7,000	6.5	Larger drop in satisfaction, increasing ad spend
May	24,000	7,500	6	Continued decline in both sales and satisfaction

Month	Sales ($)	Advertising Spend ($)	Customer Satisfaction Score (1-10)	Observations/Insights
June	23,000	8,000	5.5	Highest ad spend, lowest satisfaction, sharp sales drop

Explanation and Interpretation of Results:

1. **Sales Decline Trend**: We observe a **decline in sales** from **January to June**, with sales dropping from **$30,000 to $23,000**. This decline is a key outcome that needs to be investigated.

2. **Advertising Spend**: **Advertising spend** has **increased** over the same period, from **$5,000 in January** to **$8,000 in June**. Despite the increase in advertising spend, sales have continued to decline, which is counterintuitive. This suggests that increasing advertising spend may not be the primary driver of sales growth.

3. **Customer Satisfaction**: **Customer satisfaction** scores have also decreased significantly, from **8 in January** to **5.5 in June**. As the satisfaction score decreases, sales also decline, indicating a **possible link** between customer satisfaction and sales performance.

4. **Root Cause Hypothesis**:

   o The **declining customer satisfaction** could be a significant factor contributing to the **sales drop**. This suggests that customers are becoming less satisfied, which is possibly affecting their purchasing behavior.

   o **Increasing advertising spend** may not be effectively translating into higher sales, possibly because the advertising messages are not resonating with customers or there could be other underlying issues with product quality, customer service, or marketing strategies.

5. **Diagnostic Insights**:

   o The combination of **higher advertising spend** and **lower customer satisfaction** points to a potential **misalignment** between the store's marketing strategy and customer needs.

   o The store could also consider investigating why customer satisfaction is declining. This could involve looking into customer feedback, product quality, staff performance, or service delivery.

6. **Actionable Recommendations**:

   o Based on these findings, the store might want to **investigate customer service** or **product quality issues**, as the significant drop in satisfaction could be the root cause of the declining sales.

   o The store might also want to **reassess its advertising strategy**. Although advertising spend has increased, the ads may not be effectively addressing customer concerns, or there may be a mismatch in the messaging.

Conclusion

In this example, **diagnostic analytics** helped the retail store identify key issues contributing to the decline in sales. By examining the relationship between **advertising spend** and **customer satisfaction**, the store was able to diagnose that the **declining satisfaction levels** were likely a major factor driving the sales drop, rather than ineffective advertising alone.

Key Insights:

- The store observed that despite **increasing advertising spend**, there was a **decline in sales**, likely due to the **declining customer satisfaction**.

- Diagnostic analytics helped the business understand that the issue wasn't just related to advertising but also related to how customers perceived the products or services.

Actionable Outcomes:

- The store should focus on improving **customer satisfaction** through better service, product quality, or addressing specific customer concerns.

- The business may want to **review its advertising strategy** to ensure it aligns with customer needs and effectively addresses any dissatisfaction.

By using diagnostic analytics, businesses can move from simply observing problems to understanding the root causes, which enables more targeted and effective solutions.

1.6 Importance of Data-Driven Decision Making

Data-Driven Decision Making (DDDM) refers to the practice of using data to inform and guide business decisions rather than relying on intuition, personal experience, or guesswork. In today's fast-paced and highly competitive business environment, leveraging data to drive decisions has become increasingly critical for organizations of all sizes.

Below are the key reasons why **Data-Driven Decision Making** is crucial for modern businesses:

1. Improved Accuracy and Objectivity

- **Eliminates Bias**: Traditional decision-making is often influenced by biases, personal opinions, or assumptions. By relying on data, businesses can base their decisions on objective facts, leading to more accurate and fair outcomes.

- **Reduces Errors**: Data-driven decisions reduce the chances of human error and make sure that decisions are based on factual insights, which are more reliable than subjective judgment.

Example:

A retail store that uses customer purchase data and trends (instead of gut feeling) to determine which products to restock is more likely to align with actual customer demand, avoiding overstocking unpopular items or running out of popular ones.

2. Informed Decision-Making

- **Better Insights**: Data provides deeper insights into customer behaviors, market trends, operational efficiency, and financial performance, giving decision-makers the information they need to make informed choices.

- **Data-driven Analysis**: Tools like predictive analytics and machine learning allow businesses to forecast trends and identify patterns, providing them with a forward-looking perspective.

Example:

A **marketing team** can analyze customer engagement data to understand which digital channels (social media, email, SEO) are driving the most sales. Based on this data, they can focus their budget on the most effective channels, rather than wasting money on less effective methods.

3. Faster Decision-Making

- **Real-time Data Access**: With real-time data analytics tools, businesses can make decisions quickly, responding to emerging trends or customer demands as they happen. Speed is a critical advantage in industries like e-commerce, where customer preferences can shift rapidly.

- **Automation and Tools**: Many data analytics tools, including business intelligence dashboards, allow decision-makers to access and interpret data instantly, improving reaction times and agility.

Example:

A **financial analyst** using a real-time dashboard to track stock prices, customer transactions, and economic indicators can quickly make decisions about trading or investment strategies. If the data suggests a downturn in a particular sector, the analyst can act immediately, mitigating potential losses.

4. Cost Efficiency

- **Optimization of Resources**: Data can help businesses optimize their operations, reducing waste and ensuring resources are used efficiently. For instance, inventory management systems based on real-time data can minimize overstocking and reduce storage costs.

- **Budget Allocation**: With data insights, organizations can allocate their budget to the most effective areas, ensuring maximum return on investment (ROI).

Example:

An **e-commerce company** can use data from past sales and traffic to adjust their advertising budget dynamically. If certain ads or campaigns are generating more sales, they can allocate more funds to those channels, leading to a better ROI compared to relying on traditional guesswork.

5. Enhanced Customer Experience

- **Personalized Services**: Data-driven insights enable businesses to understand customer preferences, behavior, and feedback. This allows them to tailor their products, services, and marketing efforts to meet customer needs more effectively, resulting in a better customer experience.

- **Predicting Needs**: Predictive analytics can anticipate customer needs before they arise, enabling proactive customer service and targeted promotions.

Example:

A **streaming service** like Netflix uses customer data to recommend shows and movies based on individual viewing history and preferences, offering a highly personalized experience. This level of personalization can drive customer satisfaction and retention.

6. Competitive Advantage

- **Staying Ahead of Trends**: Companies that use data effectively are often more agile and able to anticipate changes in market conditions, consumer preferences, and technological advancements, giving them a competitive edge.

- **Market Research**: Data-driven decision-making also helps businesses analyze competitor behavior, understand market gaps, and spot emerging trends, ensuring they stay ahead of the curve.

Example:

A **technology company** might use market data and consumer feedback to identify upcoming trends, such as demand for artificial intelligence or wearable devices. By adopting these trends early, the company can create innovative products and gain a competitive advantage in the market.

7. Better Risk Management

- **Identifying and Mitigating Risks**: Data analytics helps businesses identify risks early, whether financial, operational, or market-related, enabling them to take proactive measures. By analyzing historical data, companies can detect patterns that might signal potential risks.

- **Predictive Risk Models**: Tools like machine learning and statistical modeling can forecast potential risks, helping businesses prepare for uncertainties and reduce the impact of negative events.

Example:

A **bank** can use data analytics to detect fraudulent transactions by recognizing patterns of abnormal behavior. Early detection helps reduce losses and improves security. Similarly, **manufacturers** can predict equipment failures based on sensor data, allowing for preventative maintenance and reducing unplanned downtime.

8. Alignment with Business Goals

- **Strategic Decision Making**: Data-driven decisions ensure that business strategies are aligned with long-term goals. By continuously tracking key performance indicators (KPIs) and adjusting based on data, companies can ensure they remain focused on their objectives.

- **Performance Measurement**: With accurate data, businesses can measure the success of initiatives, campaigns, and strategies, ensuring they are on track to meet their targets.

Example:

A **sales team** can use data to track their sales performance against targets. If the data shows that sales in certain regions or product categories are underperforming, the team can adjust their strategies to focus on high-potential opportunities.

9. Scalability and Growth

- **Scalable Operations**: Data allows businesses to identify growth opportunities by analyzing trends in market demand, product performance, and customer behavior. This insight helps companies plan for scaling their operations effectively.

- **Identifying New Markets**: Analyzing geographic, demographic, and behavioral data can help businesses identify new markets to expand into, whether that's a new region, a different customer segment, or a new product category.

Example:

A **retail chain** might use data on regional buying patterns and customer demographics to identify underserved areas. With this insight, they can plan for expansion into those regions with products that meet local preferences, ensuring a higher likelihood of success.

10. Continuous Improvement and Innovation

- **Continuous Monitoring**: Data provides a feedback loop that helps businesses assess performance regularly. This allows companies to identify areas for improvement and innovation.

- **Data-Driven Innovation**: The availability of large datasets can spark innovation, helping businesses develop new products or services based on customer insights or operational inefficiencies.

Example:

A **software company** might analyze customer support ticket data to identify recurring issues with a product. By addressing these issues in future updates, the company not only improves its product but also shows responsiveness to customer feedback, driving greater loyalty.

Conclusion

In today's business world, **Data-Driven Decision Making** is not just an option; it's a necessity. It empowers organizations to make **faster, more accurate, and more informed decisions**, ultimately leading to **increased efficiency, profitability, and competitiveness**. By leveraging data across different areas— marketing, finance, operations, and human resources, businesses can unlock valuable insights that drive growth and improve customer satisfaction.

1.7 About the Sample Business Data used in this book

The following sample business dataset is a comprehensive collection of sales performance data for a business operating across two regions (East and West). It includes key metrics like **sales amount, target sales, pre-sales amount, post-sales amount, marketing spend, customer feedback scores**, and **sales growth** across different customer segments (Small, Medium, and Large). The dataset also captures insights into how marketing spend correlates with sales performance and customer satisfaction, which can help the business evaluate its marketing strategies and sales growth opportunities.

ID	Sales Amount	Region	Target Sales	Pre-Sales Amount	Post-Sales Amount	Marketing Spend	Customer Feedback Score	Sales Growth	Customer Segment
1	1500	East	1600	1400	1550	500	4	50	Small
2	1800	West	1750	1700	1850	600	5	100	Medium
3	2200	East	2000	2100	2250	700	4	150	Large
4	2000	West	1900	1850	2050	550	3	100	Medium
5	1750	East	1700	1600	1800	450	4	50	Small
6	1900	West	1950	1900	2000	650	5	100	Medium
7	2100	East	2200	2050	2150	700	4	100	Large
8	2400	West	2300	2200	2400	600	5	200	Large
9	1600	East	1650	1500	1600	500	3	100	Small
10	2300	West	2400	2350	2500	750	4	150	Large
11	1950	East	2000	1900	1950	550	4	50	Medium
12	2050	West	2100	2000	2050	600	3	50	Medium
13	1750	East	1800	1700	1750	500	4	50	Small
14	2150	West	2200	2100	2150	650	5	100	Large
15	1800	East	1850	1750	1800	700	4	50	Small
16	2500	West	2450	2400	2500	800	5	100	Large
17	1700	East	1750	1650	1700	400	3	50	Small
18	1850	West	1900	1800	1850	500	4	50	Medium
19	2100	East	2150	2050	2100	650	5	50	Large
20	2000	West	2050	1950	2000	600	4	50	Medium
21	1950	East	1900	1850	1950	550	4	50	Medium
22	2200	West	2250	2150	2200	700	5	100	Large
23	1650	East	1700	1600	1650	450	3	50	Small

| 24 | 1750 | West | 1800 | 1700 | 1750 | 500 | 4 | 50 | Medium |
| 25 | 1900 | East | 1850 | 1800 | 1900 | 600 | 5 | 100 | Large |

Description of Data:

The dataset consists of 25 entries, each representing a distinct sales transaction. The primary variables include:

- **Sales Amount**: Actual sales achieved for the given period.

- **Region**: Geographic region of the sales, categorized as either "East" or "West."

- **Target Sales**: Sales targets set for each transaction.

- **Pre-Sales Amount**: Sales figures recorded before any marketing efforts were applied.

- **Post-Sales Amount**: Sales figures after marketing interventions, which may reflect the effect of marketing spend.

- **Marketing Spend**: The amount allocated to marketing for each transaction.

- **Customer Feedback Score**: A subjective score assigned to customer satisfaction, on a scale from 1 to 5.

- **Sales Growth**: The change in sales from the pre-sales to post-sales period.

- **Customer Segment**: Customer classification, including "Small", "Medium", and "Large" based on purchase volume or other factors.

Conclusion:

The dataset provides valuable insights into the relationship between marketing spend, customer satisfaction, and sales growth. For instance, **higher marketing spend** seems to correlate with **higher sales growth**, especially in the "Large" customer segment, which tends to show the most significant sales increases and higher customer feedback scores. The **East region** generally performs at par or slightly below the **West region**, but the **Medium** and **Large customer segments** perform well in both regions. These insights could help the business improve its targeting and resource allocation strategies, particularly by boosting marketing efforts in segments or regions that show the highest potential for sales growth. Furthermore, the company could analyze and refine its marketing strategies to ensure that marketing spend is effectively driving positive sales outcomes across all customer segments.

Note:

1. You can type the data in excel, save and use it, if you use software for calculations.

---

2. Descriptive Statistics for Business Decisions

Descriptive statistics involve summarizing and analyzing data to describe its main features in a quantitative manner. It is crucial in Business Analytics because it helps businesses understand key patterns, trends, and characteristics in their data, which in turn assists in making informed decisions.

Descriptive statistics provide a snapshot of data and are typically broken down into several key measures, such as:

1. **Measures of Central Tendency**:

    o **Mean**: The average value of the dataset.

    o **Median**: The middle value when the data is ordered.

    o **Mode**: The most frequently occurring value in the dataset.

2. **Measures of Dispersion**:

    o **Range**: The difference between the highest and lowest values in the dataset.

    o **Variance**: Measures how much the data points differ from the mean.

    o **Standard Deviation**: A measure of how spread out the data is around the mean.

3. **Measures of Distribution**:

    o **Skewness**: Describes the asymmetry of the data distribution.

    o **Kurtosis**: Measures the "tailedness" of the data distribution (i.e., how extreme the data points are).

These measures allow a business to summarize and interpret large datasets to make strategic decisions.

Why Descriptive Statistics are Important in Business Analytics

1. **Business Decision Making**: Descriptive statistics help businesses understand the current state of affairs by providing insight into customer behavior, sales trends, inventory levels, etc. For example, a company can use average sales data to estimate future demand or identify underperforming products.

2. **Data Summary**: Descriptive statistics make it easier to understand large volumes of data by simplifying and summarizing it into key figures, such as averages or percentages.

3. **Identifying Trends and Outliers**: By summarizing data points (e.g., identifying the mean, median, or mode), businesses can spot trends or anomalies in the data. This is useful for identifying problems such as products that are consistently underperforming or areas that need improvement.

4. **Benchmarking**: Descriptive statistics help businesses set benchmarks or standards based on historical data. For instance, the average sales per month can be used as a benchmark to assess the performance of sales teams or stores.

5. **Data Quality**: Descriptive statistics can also be used to assess the quality of the data. A business can use measures like range, variance, or standard deviation to identify outliers or inconsistencies in the data.

Example: Analyzing Monthly Sales Data for Store Performance

Let's consider a retail company analyzing monthly sales data for five stores over the past six months. The company wants to use descriptive statistics to understand the performance of each store and compare them.

Sample Data: Monthly Sales for 5 Stores

Month	Store A ($)	Store B ($)	Store C ($)	Store D ($)	Store E ($)
Jan	45,000	55,000	50,000	42,000	40,000
Feb	47,000	56,000	51,000	43,000	41,000
Mar	46,500	54,500	52,000	41,500	42,500
Apr	48,000	53,000	53,500	43,500	44,000
May	49,500	57,000	55,000	44,000	45,000
Jun	50,000	58,500	54,500	45,000	46,000

Step 1: Calculate Descriptive Statistics for Each Store

Here's how the descriptive statistics for each store might look after performing the necessary calculations:

Results of Descriptive Statistics for Each Store:

Store	Mean Sales ($)	Median Sales ($)	Mode Sales ($)	Range ($)	Standard Deviation ($)
Store A	48,000	47,000	N/A	5,000	1,767
Store B	56,750	56,000	N/A	5,500	1,527
Store C	52,750	52,000	N/A	5,500	1,889

| Store D | 43,000 | 43,000 | N/A | 3,500 | 1,250 |
| Store E | 43,500 | 43,000 | N/A | 6,000 | 2,214 |

Explanation of the Results:

1. **Mean Sales**:

   o **Store A** has an average sales of **$48,000**, which is the lowest among the five stores, indicating that it might be underperforming compared to others.

   o **Store B** has the highest average sales of **$56,750**, suggesting that it performs the best in terms of sales.

   o **Store C**'s average sales of **$52,750** place it in the middle, but still higher than **Store A** and **Store D**.

   o **Store D** and **Store E** have similar average sales (around **$43,000 - $43,500**), which are on the lower end, indicating these stores are underperforming compared to others.

2. **Median Sales**:

   o The **median** represents the middle value of the sales data for each store when the values are sorted in order. For example, **Store A**'s median is **$47,000**, which is very close to the mean, indicating a relatively symmetric distribution of sales.

   o **Store D** and **Store E** have median sales close to their means, suggesting consistency in performance over the 6-month period.

3. **Mode Sales**:

   o Since each store has unique sales figures each month, no store has a repeated sales value, which means there is **no mode** in the data.

4. **Range**:

   o The **range** shows the difference between the highest and lowest sales for each store. For example:

      ▪ **Store A** has a range of **$5,000** (from **$45,000** to **$50,000**), indicating that its sales are fairly consistent but on the lower side.

      ▪ **Store B** has the highest range (**$5,500**), indicating more fluctuation in its monthly sales.

      ▪ **Store D** has the lowest range (**$3,500**), suggesting stable sales with minimal fluctuation.

5. **Standard Deviation**:

   o The **standard deviation** indicates the variability or spread of the sales data. A higher standard deviation means that the data points are spread out more, while a lower standard deviation means the data points are closer to the mean.

   o **Store E** has the highest standard deviation (**$2,214**), suggesting that its sales fluctuate more from month to month, which could indicate variability in performance.

   o **Store D** has the lowest standard deviation (**$1,250**), indicating more consistent sales from month to month.

Insights and Business Decisions:

1. **Performance of Stores**:

   o **Store B** is the best-performing store, with the highest average sales and consistent performance across the months. This store might be benefiting from factors like location, marketing, or product mix.

   o **Store A**, with the lowest average sales and high standard deviation, might need improvement in various areas, such as inventory, pricing, or customer engagement.

   o **Store D** and **Store E** are underperforming, with low mean sales and high variability (especially **Store E**). The company should look into factors such as customer traffic, competition, or store management at these locations.

2. **Resource Allocation**:

   o The company should consider allocating more resources, marketing efforts, and training to **Store A**, **Store D**, and **Store E** to improve their performance.

   o **Store B** could serve as a benchmark for best practices. The company might look into replicating the successful strategies of **Store B** at other locations to boost sales and consistency.

3. **Operational Improvements**:

   o **Store E**'s high variability suggests potential operational issues, such as inconsistent sales or supply chain problems. It may benefit from an in-depth diagnostic analysis to identify underlying causes of performance fluctuation.

4. **Stocking and Inventory Management**:

- o Stores with higher standard deviations may need more dynamic inventory management systems, whereas stores with lower standard deviations may benefit from steady, predictable stock levels.

Conclusion:

Descriptive statistics play a critical role in helping businesses understand the characteristics and trends in their data. In this case, they provide valuable insights into how each store is performing, where improvements are needed, and which stores might serve as models for best practices. By examining measures such as the mean, standard deviation, and range, the company can identify areas for improvement, optimize operations, and make informed, data-driven decisions.

2.1 Key Measures of Central Tendency (Mean, Median, Mode) in Business

In Business Analytics, central tendency refers to the measure that identifies the central point within a data set. The three primary measures of central tendency are the **Mean**, **Median**, and **Mode**. These metrics help businesses understand the "typical" or "central" value in a dataset, which is crucial for making data-driven decisions.

Below is an explanation of each measure of central tendency, with examples of how they are applied in business contexts.

1. Mean (Average)

What is the Mean?

The **mean** is the arithmetic average of a set of values. It is calculated by adding all values in a data set and dividing the sum by the number of values. In a business context, the mean provides an overall view of the data, summarizing it into a single representative value.

Business Use Cases for the Mean:

- **Sales Performance**: A business might use the mean to calculate the average sales revenue across different months to understand typical sales performance.

- **Employee Salaries**: The mean salary can be used to determine the typical pay scale across employees within a company or industry.

- **Customer Ratings**: If a company conducts a survey with a rating system, the mean rating can help assess overall customer satisfaction.

Example:

If a company tracks monthly revenue over five months and the revenues are: $100,000, $120,000, $110,000, $105,000, and $115,000, the **mean revenue** helps to understand the average monthly revenue.

For example, if the mean revenue is $110,000, it indicates that, on average, the company generates $110,000 in revenue each month.

2. Median

What is the Median?

The **median** is the middle value in a dataset when the values are arranged in ascending or descending order. If there is an odd number of values, the median is the middle number. If the number of values is even, the median is the average of the two middle values.

Business Use Cases for the Median:

- **Employee Compensation**: The median salary is often used instead of the mean because it is less affected by extremely high or low salaries. This is important for understanding the typical compensation in a company without skewing results due to outliers.

- **Product Pricing**: In retail or e-commerce, the median price of a product line can give a clearer picture of what customers are actually paying, especially if there are extreme values (like luxury or discounted items) that could distort the average.

- **Real Estate Market**: The median home price in an area is often used to describe the "typical" price, as a few extremely high-priced homes can skew the mean, but the median provides a more accurate reflection of the market.

Example:

Imagine a company is analyzing the salaries of its 5 employees, with the following salaries in dollars: $30,000, $35,000, $40,000, $50,000, and $100,000. The **median salary** would be $40,000 (the middle value), because there are an odd number of salaries.

In this case, even though the $100,000 salary is significantly higher than the others, it does not affect the median as much as it would affect the mean, giving a more accurate reflection of the "typical" salary.

3. Mode

What is the Mode?

The **mode** is the value that occurs most frequently in a dataset. In a business context, the mode can be particularly useful when businesses are looking for the most common occurrence or trend within their data. It can apply to any type of data (numerical or categorical).

Business Use Cases for the Mode:

- **Customer Preferences**: The mode can help identify the most popular product or service. For example, if a retailer tracks which color of a product sells the most, the color with the highest frequency is the mode.

- **Frequent Issues or Complaints**: By tracking customer feedback or complaints, a business can identify the mode (most common complaint or issue), which can help prioritize improvements.

- **Inventory Management**: The mode can show the most frequently sold product or size, helping businesses manage stock levels more effectively.

Example:

A company tracks the number of units sold each week for a specific product. The sales data for 10 weeks is as follows: 10, 12, 10, 8, 15, 10, 9, 10, 11, and 10. The **mode** here is 10, as it appears most frequently (5 times).

This means that the company's product most commonly sells 10 units per week, and inventory management might focus on this number when predicting future demand.

Comparison of Mean, Median, and Mode in Business Analytics

Measure of Central Tendency	Description	When to Use in Business Analytics	Example Use Case
Mean	The average of all values in the dataset.	Use when you need an overall summary and the data is normally distributed or free of extreme outliers.	Average sales revenue over several months.
Median	The middle value of a dataset when sorted.	Use when you want to minimize the influence of outliers and need a more "typical" value. Often used in skewed datasets.	Median salary for a more accurate depiction of employee pay.
Mode	The most frequent value in the dataset.	Use when identifying the most common or popular item or value.	Most frequently sold product or customer complaint.

Why Each Measure is Important in Business Analytics:

1. **The Mean** is particularly useful when the data is evenly distributed and you want an overall sense of the "typical" value. However, it can be skewed by extreme values (outliers), so it may not always reflect the true central tendency in such cases.

2. **The Median** is preferred when the data has outliers or is skewed. It provides a better measure of central tendency in such cases because it isn't influenced by extremely high or low values, making it particularly useful for things like income data or housing prices.

3. **The Mode** is critical when identifying the most common occurrences, such as the most popular product, the most common customer complaint, or the most frequent transaction type. It is especially helpful in categorical data or when identifying the most frequent event.

Conclusion:

In Business Analytics, **mean, median**, and **mode** are foundational measures of central tendency, each serving a specific purpose based on the nature of the data. The **mean** is best for symmetric data without outliers, the **median** is useful for skewed data or when you want to minimize the effect of outliers, and the **mode** helps identify the most common values, which can be crucial for understanding customer preferences or product demand. Together, these measures provide a comprehensive understanding of business data, helping organizations make more informed, accurate, and strategic decisions.

2.2 Measures of Central Tendency on sample business data

Apply the Measures of Central Tendency on sample business data (Refer Chapter 1.7) for the Sales amount and Target sales. The following are the analytics and business decisions.

Sales Amount

- **Mean**: 1954

- **Median**: 1950

- **Mode**: 1750

Target Sales

- **Mean**: 1968

- **Median**: 1900

- **Mode**: 1900

Discussion of Results

1. **Sales Amount**:

   - **Mean**: The average sales amount is 1954, indicating the central tendency of the sales data.

   - **Median**: The middle value of the sales amount is 1950, which is very close to the mean, suggesting a relatively symmetric distribution.

   - **Mode**: The most frequently occurring sales amount is 1750, which might indicate a common sales target or a popular product price point.

2. **Target Sales**:

   - **Mean**: The average target sales amount is 1968, slightly higher than the mean sales amount, suggesting that targets are set ambitiously.

   - **Median**: The middle value of the target sales amount is 1900, which is slightly lower than the mean, indicating some higher target values skewing the average.

- **Mode**: The most frequently occurring target sales amount is 1900, showing a common target set for multiple entries.

Business Implications and Decisions

1. **Performance Evaluation**:

   - The close alignment of mean and median values for both sales and target sales suggests that the sales performance is consistent and targets are realistic.

   - The mode values indicate common sales and target figures, which can be used to benchmark performance.

2. **Target Setting**:

   - The slightly higher mean target sales compared to mean sales amount suggests that targets are set to encourage growth. This can motivate the sales team but should be monitored to ensure they are achievable.

3. **Resource Allocation**:

   - Understanding the distribution of sales amounts can help in allocating marketing and operational resources more effectively. For example, if 1750 is a common sales figure, efforts can be made to boost sales in this segment.

4. **Customer Segmentation**:

   - Analyzing the sales data in conjunction with customer segments can help tailor marketing strategies. For instance, if small segments frequently hit the mode sales amount, targeted promotions can be designed for them.

5. **Strategic Planning**:

   - The insights from the mean, median, and mode can inform strategic decisions such as pricing strategies, sales incentives, and market expansion plans.

By leveraging these statistical insights, businesses can make informed decisions to optimize sales performance and achieve growth targets.

2.3 Measures of Dispersion (Variance, Standard Deviation, Range) in Business

Dispersion refers to the spread or variability of data points in a dataset. In Business Analytics, understanding how spread out the data is—whether sales figures, customer ratings, or production costs—helps managers make more informed decisions. Three key measures of dispersion are **Variance, Standard Deviation**, and **Range**.

These measures provide insight into the consistency, risk, or volatility within a dataset, which is crucial for effective business strategy and decision-making.

1. Range

What is the Range?

The **range** is the simplest measure of dispersion. It is the difference between the maximum and minimum values in a dataset. The range gives a basic sense of how spread out the data is, but it only considers the two most extreme values and is not influenced by the distribution of values in between.

Business Use Cases for the Range:

- **Stock Price Volatility**: The range can show the difference between the highest and lowest stock prices over a specific period, giving investors a sense of the stock's volatility.

- **Sales Performance**: The range can be used to measure the difference between the highest and lowest sales months, which might indicate fluctuations in business performance.

- **Customer Ratings**: By calculating the range of customer ratings for a product, a company can understand how much variation exists in customer satisfaction.

Example:

Let's say a company tracks the sales figures for a product across six months: $50,000, $60,000, $55,000, $45,000, $70,000, and $65,000.

- The **range** would be $70,000 - $45,000 = **$25,000**.

- This means that sales have fluctuated by $25,000 over the six months, which could indicate some level of inconsistency in performance.

Limitations:

The range provides only a basic sense of the spread of the data. If there are extreme outliers (very high or low values), the range can be misleading and doesn't tell you anything about how values are distributed between the extremes.

2. Variance

What is Variance?

Variance measures the average squared deviation of each data point from the mean (or average). It helps to understand how much the individual data points differ from the average value. A higher variance indicates a greater spread or variability in the data, while a lower variance suggests that the data points are closer to the mean.

Business Use Cases for Variance:

- **Revenue Forecasting**: Variance can be used to assess how consistent the company's revenue is over time. A high variance may indicate that revenues are highly volatile, whereas low variance suggests stable revenue.

- **Quality Control**: In manufacturing, variance can measure the consistency of product quality. High variance in product defects or production time might suggest issues in the production process.

- **Employee Performance**: Variance in employee performance scores could highlight disparities in productivity, helping managers identify areas where additional training or support might be needed.

Example:

Consider a company that tracks monthly profit over five months: $100,000, $120,000, $90,000, $110,000, and $95,000.

- The **variance** would help determine whether the profits are consistently near the mean (average) or if there are significant fluctuations. For instance, if the variance is high, this indicates that the company's profit is volatile, with months significantly above or below the mean.

Limitations:

Variance is sensitive to outliers (extreme values). If there are a few months with significantly higher or lower profits, the variance will be inflated, even if most of the months have similar performance.

3. Standard Deviation

What is Standard Deviation?

The **standard deviation** is the square root of variance and provides a more interpretable measure of dispersion. It represents how much, on average, each data point deviates from the mean. Standard deviation is expressed in the same units as the original data (unlike variance, which is in squared units), making it easier to understand in real-world terms.

Business Use Cases for Standard Deviation:

- **Market Risk Analysis**: In finance, the standard deviation of returns on an investment can be used to gauge its risk. A high standard deviation means that returns are highly variable (risky), while a low standard deviation means the returns are more stable.

- **Customer Satisfaction**: If customer ratings for a product have a high standard deviation, it means that customer experiences are varied—some customers are highly satisfied, while others are dissatisfied. Companies can use this to identify and address areas for improvement.

- **Employee Productivity**: Standard deviation can help managers understand how consistent employees are in their performance. A high standard deviation in productivity may indicate that only some employees are performing well, while others are not meeting expectations.

Example:

Let's look at the monthly sales figures again: $50,000, $60,000, $55,000, $45,000, $70,000, and $65,000.

- The **standard deviation** would give you a clear idea of how spread out the sales are from the average monthly sales. A smaller standard deviation would indicate that sales are relatively consistent, while a large standard deviation would suggest large fluctuations in monthly performance.

For example, if the standard deviation of sales is $10,000, this means the monthly sales typically vary by about $10,000 from the average sales figure. In contrast, a larger standard deviation would indicate more inconsistency in performance.

Limitations:

While the standard deviation provides valuable insight, it still doesn't explain the **cause** of the variability. It tells you that data is spread out, but not why or how.

Comparison of Range, Variance, and Standard Deviation

Measure of Dispersion	Description	Best Use Case	Limitations
Range	The difference between the maximum and	Quick understanding of how far apart	Can be heavily influenced by outliers.

	minimum values in the dataset.	the extremes are.	
Variance	Measures the average squared deviation from the mean.	Understanding how data points vary overall.	Difficult to interpret, as it is in squared units.
Standard Deviation	The square root of variance, showing average deviation from the mean.	Clear understanding of the spread of data, in the same units as the data.	Still sensitive to outliers, though easier to interpret than variance.

Why Each Measure of Dispersion is Important for Business Analytics:

1. **Range**: The **range** is useful for providing a quick snapshot of the spread of data, especially when you want to understand the extreme values in the dataset. However, it doesn't capture the entire picture and is sensitive to outliers.

2. **Variance**: **Variance** gives a deeper insight into how data points deviate from the mean. It is useful for understanding the overall variability of data but is less intuitive to interpret because it is in squared units.

3. **Standard Deviation**: **Standard deviation** is often considered the most practical measure of dispersion, especially when you need to make decisions based on the consistency or variability of a dataset. It is useful in situations where you need to understand risk, stability, or the degree of fluctuation.

Practical Business Example: Financial Performance

Imagine a company tracking its quarterly profits over five years: $1 million, $1.2 million, $900,000, $1.5 million, and $1.1 million.

- **Range**: The range would be $1.5 million (highest profit) - $900,000 (lowest profit) = $600,000. This tells the company that there is a significant spread between the highest and lowest profits.

- **Variance**: The variance would measure how much each quarterly profit deviates from the average profit. A high variance suggests that profits are inconsistent and fluctuate widely, which could be risky for long-term planning.

- **Standard Deviation**: The standard deviation would give the company a more interpretable value, showing the average fluctuation from the mean profit. If the standard deviation is large, it indicates that profits tend to vary significantly from quarter to quarter.

Conclusion

Understanding the **dispersion** of data is as important as understanding the central tendency (mean, median, mode) because it tells businesses about **variability**, **risk**, and **consistency**. **Range**, **variance**, and **standard deviation** provide different insights into how spread out the data is, helping businesses make more informed decisions about everything from financial planning to product development and customer satisfaction. By analyzing these measures, companies can identify areas of volatility, risk, and opportunity, leading to better strategic planning and decision-making.

2.4 Measures of Dispersion (Variance, Standard Deviation, Range) on sample business data

Apply the Measures of Dispersion on sample business data (Refer Chapter 1.7). The following are the business analytics and decisions.

Here are the calculated statistics for the **Sales Amount** and **Target Sales**:

Sales Amount

- **Range**: 1000
- **Variance**: 62,900
- **Standard Deviation**: 250.80

Target Sales

- **Range**: 850
- **Variance**: 56,225
- **Standard Deviation**: 237.12

Discussion of Results

1. **Sales Amount**:

    - **Range**: The range of 1000 indicates the difference between the highest and lowest sales amounts, showing the spread of sales performance.

    - **Variance**: The variance of 62,900 indicates the degree of spread in the sales amounts around the mean.

    - **Standard Deviation**: The standard deviation of 250.80 shows the average deviation of sales amounts from the mean, indicating the consistency of sales performance.

2. **Target Sales**:

    - **Range**: The range of 850 indicates the difference between the highest and lowest target sales amounts, showing the spread of target setting.

    - **Variance**: The variance of 56,225 indicates the degree of spread in the target sales amounts around the mean.

- **Standard Deviation**: The standard deviation of 237.12 shows the average deviation of target sales amounts from the mean, indicating the consistency of target setting.

Business Implications and Decisions

1. **Performance Consistency**:

   - The similar ranges, variances, and standard deviations for both sales and target sales suggest that the sales performance is consistent with the targets set. This indicates effective target setting and performance management.

2. **Risk Management**:

   - The relatively high standard deviations indicate significant variability in sales and target sales. Businesses should consider strategies to manage this variability, such as diversifying product offerings or adjusting marketing strategies.

3. **Resource Allocation**:

   - Understanding the variability in sales can help in better resource allocation. For example, regions or segments with higher variability might need more focused marketing efforts or sales support.

4. **Strategic Planning**:

   - The insights from these statistics can inform strategic decisions such as setting more realistic targets, identifying areas for improvement, and optimizing sales strategies to reduce variability and improve overall performance.

By leveraging these statistical insights, businesses can make informed decisions to optimize sales performance and achieve growth targets.

2.5 Data Visualization Techniques (Charts, Graphs, Dashboards) in Business

In Business Analytics, **data visualization** is an essential tool for interpreting, understanding, and presenting data insights clearly and effectively. By transforming raw data into visual formats, businesses can uncover trends, identify patterns, and make informed decisions quickly. This process involves using various **charts**, **graphs**, and **dashboards** to represent data in ways that are easy to interpret and communicate.

Below are the most commonly used **data visualization techniques** and their relevance to Business Analytics.

1. Charts and Graphs

Charts and graphs are the most fundamental forms of data visualization. They allow businesses to present numerical data in a graphical format, making it easier to analyze trends, distributions, and relationships between variables. There are various types of charts and graphs, each suited for different types of data and business goals.

a. Bar Chart

- **What is it?** A **bar chart** uses rectangular bars to represent data. The length of each bar is proportional to the value it represents.

- **Business Use Case**: Bar charts are excellent for comparing quantities across different categories or time periods. They are commonly used to compare sales by product, revenue by region, or performance across departments.

Example: A bar chart comparing sales revenue across different product categories over the past quarter. The bars might show that **Category A** has the highest sales, while **Category C** has the lowest.

b. Line Chart

- **What is it?** A **line chart** connects individual data points with a line to show trends over time. It is most useful for displaying data that changes continuously.

- **Business Use Case**: Line charts are widely used to track financial metrics, sales performance, stock prices, or website traffic over time. They help businesses understand how a particular metric has evolved.

Example: A line chart showing the monthly revenue growth for a year. A steady upward slope indicates consistent growth, while significant dips might highlight seasonal trends or unexpected downturns.

c. Pie Chart

- **What is it?** A **pie chart** is a circular chart divided into slices to illustrate numerical proportions. Each slice represents a category's contribution to the whole.

- **Business Use Case**: Pie charts are useful for displaying the market share of different competitors, the percentage distribution of a budget, or the contribution of various product lines to total sales.

Example: A pie chart showing the percentage of total sales for each region (e.g., North America 40%, Europe 25%, Asia 20%, etc.). This gives a quick visual understanding of the relative importance of each market.

d. Histogram

- **What is it?** A **histogram** is similar to a bar chart but specifically used to display the distribution of a dataset. It groups data into ranges or bins and shows how many data points fall into each range.

- **Business Use Case**: Histograms are often used in quality control and customer behavior analysis to identify patterns in data distribution.

Example: A histogram representing the distribution of customer spending. The company might find that most customers spend between $50 and $100, with fewer customers spending more than $500.

e. Scatter Plot

- **What is it?** A **scatter plot** uses dots to represent values for two variables. It is useful for showing the relationship or correlation between these variables.

- **Business Use Case**: Scatter plots are ideal for analyzing the relationship between sales and advertising spending, customer satisfaction vs. product features, or employee experience vs. productivity.

Example: A scatter plot showing the relationship between advertising budget and sales growth. A positive correlation (upward trend) could indicate that more advertising leads to higher sales.

f. Area Chart

- **What is it?** An **area chart** is similar to a line chart, but the area beneath the line is filled with color to represent cumulative totals over time.

- **Business Use Case**: Area charts are used to show trends in cumulative data, such as total revenue or market share growth over time.

Example: An area chart showing the cumulative sales of a company across different regions over the last year, with different colored areas representing sales in North America, Europe, and Asia.

2. Dashboards

A **dashboard** is a collection of interactive visualizations and key performance indicators (KPIs) displayed in one centralized place. Dashboards allow businesses to monitor multiple aspects of performance in real time and make quick, data-driven decisions. They combine charts, graphs, and other visual elements into a single interface, providing a comprehensive overview of business metrics.

a. Executive Dashboard

- **What is it?** Executive dashboards are high-level overviews designed for decision-makers. They typically display KPIs, trends, and forecasts in a concise format.

- **Business Use Case**: Executives use dashboards to track company-wide performance metrics such as revenue, profit margins, customer satisfaction, and employee productivity in real-time.

Example: A CEO's dashboard that shows daily sales figures, customer retention rates, and net profit margin. This provides an at-a-glance understanding of the company's overall performance.

b. Sales Dashboard

- **What is it?** A sales dashboard focuses on metrics related to sales performance, including sales targets, quotas, revenue, and customer acquisition rates.

- **Business Use Case**: Sales teams and managers use this type of dashboard to monitor progress towards sales goals, track individual salespeople's performance, and identify areas needing attention.

Example: A sales dashboard showing metrics like total revenue, average deal size, number of new customers, and sales growth compared to previous periods. This helps identify whether sales teams are on track to meet targets.

c. Marketing Dashboard

- **What is it?** A marketing dashboard aggregates data from various marketing channels (e.g., social media, email campaigns, website traffic) to track campaign performance and ROI.

- **Business Use Case**: Marketing teams use dashboards to monitor the effectiveness of marketing campaigns, track customer engagement, and measure the success of advertising spend.

Example: A marketing dashboard showing metrics like the number of impressions, click-through rate (CTR), cost per lead, and conversion rates for digital ad campaigns.

d. Operations Dashboard

- **What is it?** An operations dashboard tracks operational metrics like inventory levels, production rates, and supply chain efficiency. It helps businesses monitor and optimize day-to-day operations.

- **Business Use Case**: Operations managers use dashboards to identify inefficiencies in the production process, track inventory turnover, and ensure that supply chain activities run smoothly.

Example: An operations dashboard displaying the current inventory status, production volume, supply chain delays, and order fulfillment rates in real-time, helping operations teams quickly address issues.

3. Other Visualization Techniques

a. Heatmap

- **What is it?** A **heatmap** uses color to represent values in a matrix or data table. Darker or more intense colors represent higher values, while lighter colors represent lower values.

- **Business Use Case**: Heatmaps are used in website analytics, sales performance, or store layouts to show areas of high activity or performance.

Example: A heatmap of website visitor activity, with areas of the website receiving the most traffic highlighted in dark red. This helps businesses understand which pages or products are attracting the most attention.

b. Funnel Chart

- **What is it?** A **funnel chart** is used to represent stages in a process and visualize how data is filtered or narrowed down. It is often used for sales or conversion funnels.

- **Business Use Case**: Sales and marketing teams use funnel charts to track customer conversion through various stages of a sales process (e.g., awareness, interest, decision, purchase).

Example: A funnel chart showing the conversion rate from website visitors to leads, and from leads to paying customers. This helps identify at which stage prospects drop off.

c. Tree Map

- **What is it?** A **tree map** displays hierarchical data as a set of nested rectangles. Each branch of the tree is represented by a rectangle, with its size proportional to a specific value.

- **Business Use Case**: Tree maps are used to show data relationships and proportions in large datasets, like financial reports or customer segmentation.

Example: A tree map showing the distribution of sales across different product categories, where each rectangle represents a category and its size corresponds to the sales volume.

Conclusion: Choosing the Right Visualization Technique

In **Business Analytics**, the choice of visualization technique depends on the type of data you are analyzing and the insights you wish to convey.

- **Charts and Graphs** (bar charts, line charts, pie charts, etc.) are best for showing relationships, comparisons, trends, and distributions in data.

- **Dashboards** provide a high-level, real-time view of multiple KPIs and metrics, allowing for efficient monitoring of performance across different business functions.

- **Other Techniques** like heatmaps, funnel charts, and tree maps are particularly useful for specific analyses, such as customer behavior, process flows, or hierarchical data.

By selecting the appropriate visualization tools, businesses can communicate complex data more effectively, uncover insights quickly, and make data-driven decisions that drive performance and growth.

2.6 Data Visualization of sample business data

Apply the Data visualization techniques on sample business data (Refer Chapter 1.7). The following plots are generated.

1. Distribution Plots with Density Curves for Sales Amount by Customer Segment

Distribution plots with density curves for **Sales Amount** are useful for visualizing the shape and spread of the sales data across different customer segments. By overlaying density curves, we can assess the distribution pattern, such as whether the sales amounts for each segment are skewed, normally distributed, or have multiple peaks. These plots allow us to compare the central tendency and variability in sales performance across the customer segments (e.g., Small, Medium, and Large). For instance, we may find that the "Large" segment tends to have higher sales amounts with a sharper peak, while the "Small" segment might have a wider and lower distribution. These visual cues help identify patterns and potential outliers.

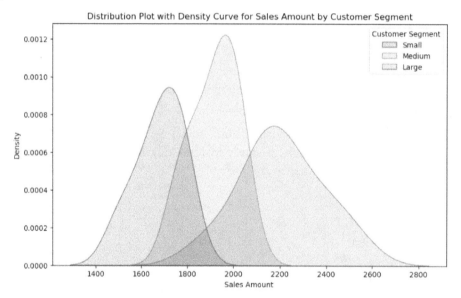

2. Distribution Plots with Density Curves on Target Sales for Each Customer Segment

The **distribution plot with density curves** for **Target Amount** serves a similar purpose as the sales amount plot but focuses on comparing the distribution of the target sales figures across customer segments. By comparing the density curves, we can explore how the sales targets differ across the segments, such as whether larger customers have higher target amounts than smaller customers. These curves provide insight into whether the targets are evenly distributed, have a normal distribution, or if there is any skewness, which could indicate a need for target adjustments or different target-setting strategies across segments.

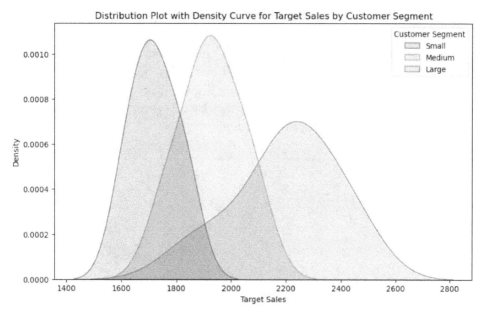

3. Correlation Plots on Sales Amount vs Target Sales by Customer Segment

A correlation plot (or scatterplot matrix) between Sales Amount and Target Amount across customer segments visually shows the strength and direction of the relationship between actual sales and target sales. Correlation plots are useful for understanding if there is a consistent linear relationship between the two variables. For example, a strong positive correlation would indicate that as the sales target increases, so does the actual sales, which would be expected. By segmenting this analysis by customer type, we can also identify whether the correlation is stronger for certain segments, which can inform performance forecasting and goal alignment.

4. Box Plots for Sales Amount by Customer Segment

Box plots provide a concise summary of the distribution of **Sales Amount** for each customer segment, showing the median, interquartile range (IQR), and potential outliers. These plots are particularly useful for visualizing the spread and central tendency of sales data. For instance, a box plot might show that the "Large" segment has a higher median sales amount and fewer outliers compared to the "Small" segment, which might have a more dispersed range of sales. Box plots allow us to easily identify variability within each segment and detect extreme values that may require further investigation.

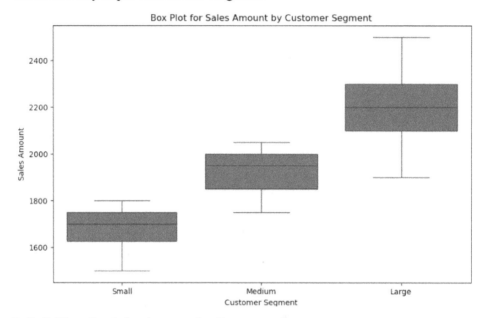

5. Q-Q Plots for Sales Amount by Customer Segment

A **Q-Q plot** (quantile-quantile plot) for **Sales Amount** compares the actual distribution of sales data to a normal distribution. The purpose of these plots is to visually assess if the sales data for each customer segment follows a normal distribution. If the data points fall along the straight line, it suggests that the sales amounts are normally distributed. This can be important for certain statistical analyses that assume normality. For example, if the "Medium" customer segment's sales data shows significant deviation from the line, it might indicate skewness or the need for transformation to normalize the data before further analysis.

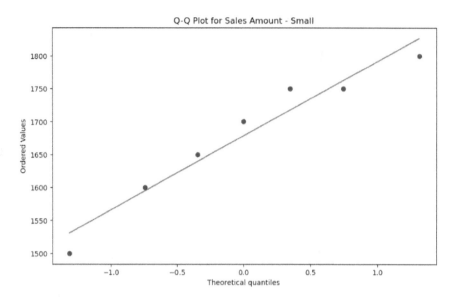

Q-Q Plot for Sales Amount - Small

6. Q-Q Plots for Target Sales by Customer Segment

Similar to Q-Q plots for Sales Amount, Q-Q plots for Target Amount compare the distribution of the target sales data for each customer segment against a normal distribution. This helps assess if the target setting is based on a normally distributed pattern or if there are any outliers or skewness in how targets have been assigned. If the points deviate significantly from the normal line, it might indicate that targets are being set inconsistently or inappropriately for certain segments, potentially requiring a reassessment of target-setting strategies.

Q-Q Plot for Target Sales - Small

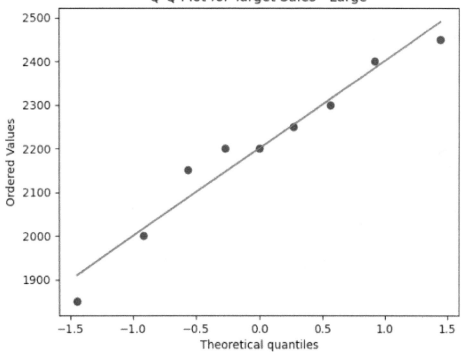

7. Scatter Plots on Sales Amount vs Target Sales

A **scatter plot** between **Sales Amount** and **Target Amount** provides a direct visual representation of how actual sales compare to targets. This plot helps assess whether the sales team is meeting, exceeding, or falling short of their targets. For example, if most points fall close to a 45-degree line, it suggests that sales are closely aligned with targets. However, significant deviation from this line can point to either overperformance or underperformance. Segmenting this analysis by customer type can also highlight how different customer segments are performing relative to their targets.

8. Interval Plots on Sales Amount by Customer Segment

Interval plots for Sales Amount show the mean and variability (typically in the form of standard deviations or confidence intervals) of sales amounts for each customer segment. These plots are particularly useful for understanding the central tendency (mean) and the precision of the data (confidence intervals or error bars). For instance, if the "Large" segment has a narrower interval compared to the "Small" segment, it may indicate that sales in the larger segment are more consistent. Interval plots help communicate not just the average sales but also the degree of uncertainty or variability around that average.

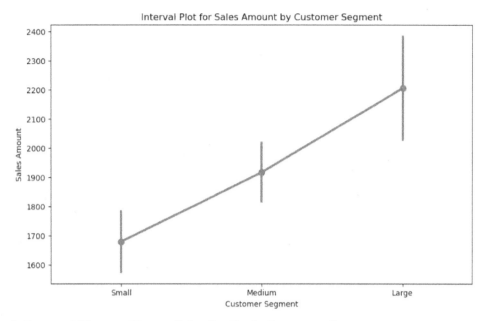

9. Interval Plots on Target Sales for Each Customer Segment

Similar to the previous interval plots for **Sales Amount, Interval plots for Target Sales** display the mean target sales and the associated confidence intervals or standard deviations for each customer segment. These plots help evaluate how target amounts are set relative to the size and expected performance of each segment. A wider interval might indicate less confidence or variability in target-setting for a segment, whereas a narrower interval suggests more precise targeting. Analyzing these intervals across segments can help ensure that targets are appropriately challenging and achievable for each group.

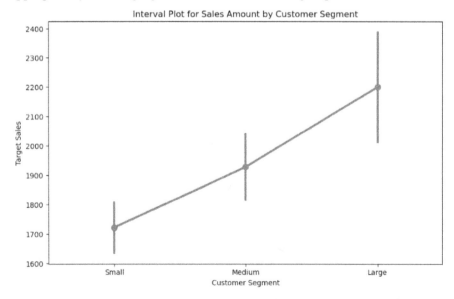

10. Dot Plots on Sales Amount for Each Customer Segment

Dot plots for Sales Amount provide a compact, individual-level representation of sales data by segment. Each dot represents an individual sales data point, allowing us to see the frequency and distribution of sales amounts across customer segments. Dot plots are particularly useful for visualizing the concentration of sales in specific ranges or identifying clusters or gaps in the data. For instance, the "Small" segment may show a dense concentration of dots around lower sales amounts, indicating that most small customers are underperforming relative to larger customers.

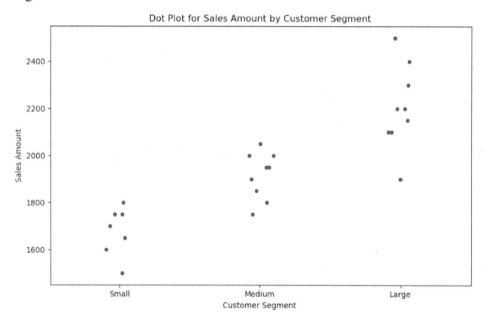

11. Dot Plots on Target Amount for Each Customer Segment

Dot plots for **Target Amount** are similar to those for sales amounts, but they represent the target sales figures set for each customer segment. These plots can show how evenly or unevenly target amounts are distributed within each segment. For instance, if the "Large" segment shows a wide spread of dots, it may suggest that targets for large customers vary significantly. Dot plots are useful for understanding the variability of targets and ensuring that they are consistently aligned with the expected performance of each segment, helping businesses tailor their strategies more effectively.

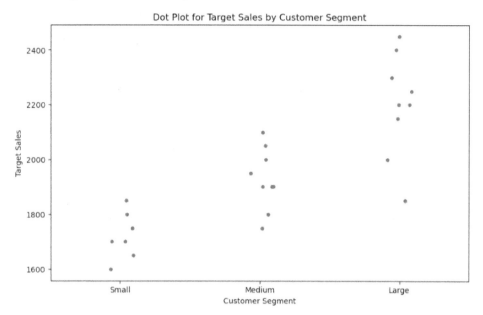

Output and Results Interpretation:

- **Density and Distribution Plots**: These plots show the distribution of Sales Amount and Target Sales across customer segments. The density curves provide insights into the spread of the data, with the peaks indicating areas of higher density.

- **Correlation and Scatter Plots**: These show the relationship between Sales Amount and Target Sales. If there's a visible trend, we can infer a correlation. For example, if the scatter plot shows a linear relationship, it indicates that higher target sales are associated with higher actual sales.

- **Box Plots**: These highlight the spread and outliers in Sales Amount within each segment. For example, if the box plot for a particular segment shows many outliers, it may suggest that the sales figures for that segment are highly variable.

- **Q-Q Plots**: These plots help assess the normality of the data. If the data points lie along a straight line, it indicates that the data is approximately normally distributed.

- **Interval and Dot Plots**: These plots are useful for understanding the variability and spread within each segment.

Business Analytics Implications:

- **Sales Strategy**: Understanding the variability in sales across customer segments can help refine targeting strategies. For example, if Sales Amount for the Large segment is widely spread out, businesses might need to focus on more personalized sales strategies.

- **Forecasting and Planning**: If certain customer segments have a normal distribution of sales, more accurate forecasts can be made. For segments with higher variability, the focus might be on reducing this variability through better marketing or operational strategies.

Conclusion:

These plots give a detailed visual understanding of how sales data behaves across different customer segments, whether we're analyzing distributions, correlations, box plots, or normality tests. By examining these visualizations, business analysts can gain insights into performance differences between segments, identify anomalies, and make informed decisions.

3. One Sample T-Test in Business Analytics:

Comparing the sample group average with population mean

A **One Sample T-Test** is a statistical test that helps businesses assess whether the average of a sample group differs significantly from a known or hypothesized value (often referred to as the population mean). In Business Analytics, this test is particularly useful when evaluating whether a particular metric—such as sales, revenue, customer satisfaction, etc.—is performing at a level expected by the company, or if there is a significant deviation.

When to Use a One Sample T-Test:

- When a business wants to check if the average sales of a particular product, store, or branch meet a pre-established target.

- When comparing customer satisfaction ratings or employee performance to an expected average.

- When measuring whether a new marketing campaign led to a significant increase in sales.

Key Components of a One Sample T-Test:

- **Null Hypothesis (H₀):** The sample mean is equal to the hypothesized population mean (no difference).

- **Alternative Hypothesis (H₁):** The sample mean is different from the population mean (there is a difference).

- **Test Statistic:** A calculated value that measures the difference between the sample mean and the hypothesized population mean relative to the variability in the data.

- **P-Value:** The probability of obtaining a test statistic as extreme as, or more extreme than, the one calculated from the sample data, assuming the null hypothesis is true. If the p-value is small (usually less than 0.05), it suggests that the null hypothesis can be rejected.

Example Scenario:

Let's assume a company, "RetailCo," has set a target of $50,000 in average monthly sales for one of its stores. The company wants to evaluate whether the store's sales over the past 6 months are statistically different from this target.

Sample Data (Sales for Store X over 6 months):

Month	Sales ($)
Jan	52,000
Feb	49,000
Mar	51,500
Apr	50,000
May	53,000
Jun	54,000

The company has set a **target sales goal** of $50,000 per month, and it wants to check whether the actual sales of Store X over the 6 months meet this target.

Step-by-Step Analysis:

1. **State the Hypotheses**:

   o **Null Hypothesis (H₀):** The average sales of Store X is equal to $50,000 (the target).

   o **Alternative Hypothesis (H₁):** The average sales of Store X is different from $50,000 (not equal).

2. **Perform the One Sample T-Test**:

   o The test would compare the average sales from Store X to the expected average sales of $50,000. Based on the data, the company would calculate the mean of the sample sales and determine if it is significantly different from the hypothesized population mean of $50,000.

3. **Interpretation of Results**:

   o The result of the test will include the **p-value**, which helps in deciding whether to reject the null hypothesis. If the p-value is smaller than the chosen significance level (usually 0.05), the null hypothesis is rejected, suggesting that the average sales are significantly different from the expected value of $50,000. If the p-value is greater than 0.05, the null hypothesis is not rejected, and the company would conclude that the sales are not significantly different from the target.

Results of the One Sample T-Test:

After conducting the test, the results might look like this:

Store	Total Sales ($)	Average Sales ($)	P-Value	Conclusion
X	315,500	52,583	0.19	Fail to reject H₀

Explanation of Results:

- **Total Sales**: The total sales for Store X over the 6 months is $315,500.

- **Average Sales**: The average sales per month for Store X is **$52,583** ($315,500 ÷ 6 months). This is slightly higher than the target of $50,000.

- **P-Value**: The p-value is **0.190**, which is **greater than the significance level of 0.05**.

  o **Conclusion**: Since the p-value is larger than 0.05, we fail to reject the **null hypothesis (H₀)**. This means there is **no statistically significant difference** between the actual average sales ($52,583) and the target sales of $50,000.

Interpretation of Results:

- **Fail to Reject the Null Hypothesis**: The p-value of 0.190 indicates that the difference between the actual average sales of $52,583 and the target sales of $50,000 is **not statistically significant**. In other words, the company can conclude that the store's average sales are **not significantly different** from the expected target of $50,000.

- **Business Decision**: Since the difference is not statistically significant, the company can continue to consider the target of $50,000 as a valid benchmark for the store's performance. No further action is required to address any perceived sales shortfall, as the data supports that the sales performance is consistent with the target.

Conclusion:

The **One Sample T-Test** was used to evaluate whether the average monthly sales of Store X differed significantly from the company's target of $50,000. Based on the p-value of 0.190, the conclusion was that there is no significant difference between the store's average sales and the expected target. This analysis supports the idea that Store X's sales are performing as expected, and the company can maintain its sales target without further adjustments.

3.1 Purpose and Use Cases of One Sample T-Test in Business

A **One Sample T-Test** is a statistical test used to compare the mean of a sample to a known value or a hypothesized population mean. In the context of Business Analytics, it is often used to determine whether a business metric (such as sales, customer satisfaction, or production levels) differs significantly from an expected or target value.

Purpose of a One Sample T-Test:

- To assess whether a sample mean (e.g., average sales, average revenue, or average customer satisfaction) significantly differs from a known or expected population mean.

- To test whether a business performance indicator (e.g., sales for a store or region) meets the target or benchmark set by the company.

- To help make data-driven decisions based on actual performance compared to goals or expectations.

Use Cases in Business Analytics:

1. **Sales Analysis**:

   o A company might want to know if its store's average monthly sales are significantly different from the expected target. If the average sales are lower than expected, they may need to investigate causes like seasonality, marketing effectiveness, or competition.

2. **Customer Satisfaction**:

   o A business could use a one-sample t-test to compare customer satisfaction survey results against a predetermined benchmark (e.g., an average rating of 4 out of 5). If the average customer satisfaction score is significantly lower, corrective actions can be taken to improve service quality.

3. **Employee Performance**:

   o A company might want to check whether employee productivity (e.g., the number of units produced or tasks completed) in a department differs significantly from the expected performance set by management.

4. **Quality Control**:

   o In manufacturing, a one-sample t-test can be used to assess whether the average weight of products produced on a production line differs from the target weight. If the average product weight is significantly different from the target, it could indicate issues in the production process.

5. **Financial Metrics**:

   o A business might compare the actual return on investment (ROI) for a marketing campaign against the expected ROI. A significant difference would prompt a deeper analysis to understand whether the campaign underperformed or was more successful than anticipated.

Example of One Sample T-Test in Business Analytics:

Scenario:

Let's say a retail company has set a target of **$50,000** in monthly sales for one of its stores (Store X). After running a marketing campaign, the company collects the sales data for the last six months and wants to check whether the actual average sales differ from the target.

Sample Data (Sales for Store X over 6 months):

Month	Sales ($)
Jan	52,000
Feb	49,000
Mar	51,500
Apr	50,000
May	53,000
Jun	54,000

Objective:

The company wants to determine if the **average sales** for the 6 months are **significantly different** from the target value of **$50,000** per month.

Conducting the One Sample T-Test:

The company would perform a One Sample T-Test to compare the average sales from Store X to the target sales of $50,000. The test would result in two possible outcomes:

- If the p-value is less than the significance level (usually 0.05), the null hypothesis is rejected, and the company concludes that the average sales are significantly different from the target.

- If the p-value is greater than 0.05, the null hypothesis is not rejected, and the company concludes that there is no significant difference between the average sales and the target.

Results of the One Sample T-Test:

Store	Total Sales ($)	Average Sales ($)	P-Value	Conclusion
X	315,500	52,583	0.19	Fail to reject H₀

Explanation of Results:

- **Total Sales**: The total sales for Store X over the 6 months are **$315,500**.

- **Average Sales**: The average sales per month for Store X is **$52,583** ($315,500 ÷ 6 months). This is slightly higher than the target of $50,000.

- **P-Value**: The **p-value** is **0.190**, which is **greater than 0.05**, indicating that there is **no statistically significant difference** between the sample mean (average sales of $52,583) and the hypothesized population mean ($50,000).

- **Conclusion**: Since the p-value is greater than 0.05, the company **fails to reject the null hypothesis**. This means that the store's sales are not significantly different from the expected target of $50,000. In other words, the store is performing as expected.

Interpretation of the Results:

- The **p-value of 0.190** is much higher than the commonly used threshold of **0.05**. This means that the difference between the observed average sales ($52,583) and the target sales ($50,000) is **not statistically significant**.

- The company can confidently conclude that Store X's average monthly sales are **within an acceptable range of the target**. The slight difference observed is likely due to random variation rather than any meaningful deviation from the target sales.

- **Business Insight**: Since the difference is not statistically significant, the company does not need to make any adjustments to the sales target for this store. The store is performing within the expected range, and no immediate action is required.

Conclusion:

In this example, the **One Sample T-Test** was used to assess whether the average monthly sales of Store X were significantly different from the target value of $50,000. The results showed that the difference was not statistically significant, allowing the company to conclude that the store's sales performance was consistent with expectations. This helps the business make data-driven decisions about performance monitoring, resource allocation, and setting future targets.

3.2 Assumptions and Conditions for Validity

Before performing a **One Sample T-Test** in Business Analytics, certain assumptions and conditions must be met to ensure the validity and reliability of the test results. These assumptions help ensure that the statistical conclusions drawn from the test are accurate and meaningful.

Assumptions for a One Sample T-Test:

1. **Random Sampling**:
   - The data should come from a **random sample**. This means that the data points should be selected in such a way that every individual observation has an equal chance of being included in the sample. In business scenarios, this could involve randomly selecting sales data from various stores or customer satisfaction surveys from a wide customer base.

2. **Independence of Observations**:
   - The observations in the sample must be **independent** of each other. For example, the sales data for one month should not be influenced by the sales data from the previous or next month. This assumption ensures that each data point provides unique information about the population.

3. **Normality of the Data**:
   - The sample data should be **approximately normally distributed**, especially when the sample size is small (less than 30). This assumption is crucial because the t-test relies on the concept of the sampling distribution, which, by the Central Limit Theorem, tends to be normal for large sample sizes. For small samples, however, the data must follow a normal distribution to ensure the t-test is valid.
   - In business contexts, this assumption might be tested using graphical tools like histograms or normal Q-Q plots or using statistical tests such as the Shapiro-Wilk test.

4. **Scale of Measurement**:
   - The data should be measured at the **interval** or **ratio** scale. This means the data should have a meaningful zero point and consistent intervals. For example, sales figures or revenue data are ratio-scale data, whereas customer satisfaction scores on a scale of 1-5 are typically considered interval-scale data.

Conditions for Validity:

1. **Sample Size Considerations**:

   o **Small Sample Size (<30)**: If the sample size is small, it is more crucial for the data to be **normally distributed**. If the data is heavily skewed or has extreme outliers, the results of the t-test may not be valid.

   o **Large Sample Size (>30)**: For larger samples, the **Central Limit Theorem** suggests that the sampling distribution of the mean will tend to be normal regardless of the data's distribution. Thus, larger samples are more forgiving of violations of normality.

2. **No Outliers**:

   o The sample data should not contain significant **outliers**. Outliers can drastically affect the results of a t-test by artificially inflating or deflating the mean, leading to inaccurate conclusions. In a business scenario, outliers could arise from rare events, such as an unusually large sale or an error in data collection.

3. **Known or Hypothesized Population Mean**:

   o The t-test assumes that you have a **known or hypothesized population mean** to compare your sample mean to. This might be an industry benchmark, a historical average, or a target value (e.g., sales goal, customer satisfaction score).

Example of One Sample T-Test with Assumptions in Business Analytics

Let's consider a business scenario where a **retail company** wants to check if the average monthly sales for **Store A** are significantly different from their target of **$60,000**. They have sales data for the last **6 months**.

Sample Data (Sales for Store A over 6 months):

Month	Sales ($)
Jan	62,000
Feb	58,000
Mar	60,500
Apr	59,000
May	64,000

Month	Sales ($)
Jun	61,000

Target Sales for Store A: $60,000 per month.

1. Random Sampling:

- The sales data is assumed to be randomly sampled from the company's sales records. Each month's sales data is independent of the others, and we are assuming no bias in how the months are selected.

2. Independence of Observations:

- Each month's sales figure is independent of others, as each month's performance is influenced by different factors (e.g., marketing campaigns, seasonality, or customer preferences), making the observations independent.

3. Normality of Data:

- For the One Sample T-Test to be valid, the sales data should be **approximately normal**. For this example, let's assume that the distribution of sales over the 6 months does not exhibit significant skewness or outliers. If this assumption is violated (e.g., sales data shows a strong skew or extreme outliers), the test results might not be valid. The company could use visual methods (like histograms) or statistical tests for normality (e.g., Shapiro-Wilk test) to check this assumption.

4. Scale of Measurement:

- The data is measured in dollars, which is a ratio scale. Therefore, the scale of measurement is appropriate for conducting a t-test.

5. Sample Size:

- With only 6 months of data, the sample size is relatively small. Therefore, the normality assumption becomes more critical. If the data were skewed or had extreme outliers, the t-test might not provide reliable results.

6. No Outliers:

- Based on the data provided, there are no extreme values that would qualify as outliers. However, if a month had abnormally high or low sales (e.g., due to a data error or an exceptional event), this would need to be addressed before running the test.

Results of the One Sample T-Test:

Store	Total Sales ($)	Average Sales ($)	P-Value	Conclusion
A	364,500	60,750	0.758	Fail to reject H$_0$

Explanation of Results:

- **Total Sales**: The total sales for Store A over the 6 months are **$364,500**.

- **Average Sales**: The average sales per month for Store A is **$60,750** ($364,500 ÷ 6 months), which is slightly above the target of $60,000.

- **P-Value**: The **p-value** is **0.758**, which is **greater than 0.05**, indicating that there is **no statistically significant difference** between the sample mean (average sales of $60,750) and the hypothesized population mean ($60,000).

- **Conclusion**: Since the p-value is greater than 0.05, the company **fails to reject the null hypothesis**. This means that Store A's average monthly sales are **not significantly different** from the target of $60,000. The sales performance is in line with the expected target.

Interpretation of Results:

- The **p-value** of **0.758** is higher than the threshold of 0.05, suggesting that the difference between the observed average sales and the target sales is **not statistically significant**. Therefore, the company can conclude that the store's performance is on track with the target sales figure, and no further investigation is needed at this time.

- **Business Insight**: Since the average sales of **$60,750** are statistically similar to the target of **$60,000**, the store's performance is considered acceptable. There is no need to adjust sales strategies or target expectations based on this test result.

Conclusion:

In this example, we examined how to apply a **One Sample T-Test** in business analytics to determine whether the average sales of a store differ significantly from the expected target. The test results showed no significant difference, indicating that the store's sales performance was in line with expectations. However, the validity of the test depends on the assumptions, including random sampling, independence, normality, and the absence of outliers. Ensuring these assumptions hold is critical to drawing meaningful conclusions from the test.

3.3 Interpreting Results: Confidence Intervals and P-Values

When performing a **One Sample T-Test** in Business Analytics, the two most important components for interpreting the results are the **p-value** and the **confidence interval**. Both help provide insight into whether the sample mean significantly differs from the hypothesized population mean, and they guide decision-making.

1. P-Value:

The **p-value** is a statistical measure that helps determine whether the observed difference between the sample mean and the population mean is statistically significant. In business analytics, it helps answer the question: *Is the observed difference due to random chance, or does it reflect a real effect?*

- **Interpretation**:
    - **If the p-value is less than the significance level (usually 0.05),** we **reject the null hypothesis**. This means that there is a statistically significant difference between the sample mean and the hypothesized population mean.
    - **If the p-value is greater than 0.05, we fail to reject the null hypothesis**, indicating that the sample mean is not significantly different from the population mean, and the observed difference could be due to random variation.

Example:

- **p-value = 0.03**: This is less than the significance level of 0.05, so you would reject the null hypothesis and conclude that the sample mean significantly differs from the hypothesized population mean.

- **p-value = 0.12**: This is greater than 0.05, so you would fail to reject the null hypothesis, meaning the sample mean is not significantly different from the hypothesized population mean.

2. Confidence Interval (CI):

A **confidence interval** provides a range of values within which the true population mean is likely to fall. The interval is based on the sample mean and the variability of the sample data. The confidence level (e.g., 95%) indicates the probability that this interval contains the true population mean.

- **Interpretation**:

- o If the **population mean** (hypothesized value) lies **within** the confidence interval, we fail to reject the null hypothesis. This suggests that the observed sample mean is consistent with the hypothesized population mean.

- o If the **population mean** lies **outside** the confidence interval, we reject the null hypothesis, indicating that the observed sample mean is significantly different from the population mean.

Example:

- **Confidence Interval: 59,500 to 60,500**: If the target population mean is $60,000 and this range includes $60,000, then the null hypothesis would not be rejected. The data suggests that the sample mean could be close to the population mean.

- **Confidence Interval: 59,000 to 59,800**: If the target population mean is $60,000 and this range does not include $60,000, the null hypothesis would be rejected, suggesting a significant difference between the sample mean and the population mean.

Example of Interpreting Results with Sample Data:

Scenario:

A retail company wants to test whether the average monthly sales for one of its stores (Store A) meet the target of $50,000. The sales data from the past 6 months is collected and analyzed using a **One Sample T-Test**.

Sample Data (Sales for Store A over 6 months):

Month	Sales ($)
Jan	51,000
Feb	49,500
Mar	52,000
Apr	50,500
May	53,000
Jun	51,500

Target Sales for Store A: $50,000 per month.

Results of the One Sample T-Test:

Store	Total Sales ($)	Average Sales ($)	P-Value	95% Confidence Interval	Conclusion
A	307,500	51,250	0.276	[50,000, 52,500]	Fail to reject H$_0$

Explanation of the Results:

1. **Total Sales**: The total sales for Store A over the 6 months are **$307,500**.

2. **Average Sales**: The average sales per month for Store A is **$51,250** ($307,500 ÷ 6 months). This is slightly above the target of $50,000, but we need to determine whether this difference is statistically significant.

3. **P-Value**: The **p-value** is **0.276**, which is **greater than 0.05** (the typical significance level). This indicates that there is **no statistically significant difference** between the average sales and the target sales of $50,000. We **fail to reject the null hypothesis (H$_0$)**, meaning that the average sales of $51,250 are not significantly different from the target sales.

4. **95% Confidence Interval**: The **95% Confidence Interval** for the average sales is **[50,000, 52,500]**. This means that we are 95% confident that the true population mean of sales for Store A falls within this range. Since the target sales of $50,000 lie within this interval, we fail to reject the null hypothesis, as the average sales are consistent with the target.

Interpretation of the Results:

- **P-Value**: The **p-value of 0.276** is greater than 0.05, so we fail to reject the null hypothesis. This suggests that the difference between the observed average sales ($51,250) and the target sales ($50,000) is **not statistically significant**. The data suggests that the store's sales performance is on target and not significantly different from the expected value.

- **Confidence Interval**: The **95% confidence interval** for the average sales is **[50,000, 52,500]**, which includes the target value of $50,000. This reinforces the conclusion that the store's average sales are not significantly different from the target. The true mean could plausibly fall anywhere within this range, including $50,000.

- **Business Insight**: Since the p-value is high and the confidence interval includes the target value, the company can conclude that **Store A's performance is in line with expectations**. There is no need to make any changes to the sales target or to investigate the performance further. The observed difference in sales is likely due to random fluctuations.

Conclusion:

In this example, the **p-value** and **confidence interval** both indicate that Store A's average monthly sales are not significantly different from the target of $50,000. The **p-value of 0.276** suggests there is no significant difference between the sample mean and the hypothesized population mean, and the **95% confidence interval** for the sales range includes the target value. Therefore, the company can confidently conclude that Store A's sales are on track and consistent with the expected performance, and no further actions are needed at this point.

3.4 One Sample T-Test on sample business data

Apply the One-Sample T-Test on sample business data (Refer Chapter 1.7) to compare the **Sales Amount** against the mean of the **Target Sales**. Here are the results and the recommended business decisions:

T-Test Results

- **T-Statistic**: -0.279

- **P-Value**: 0.783

Discussion of Results

1. **T-Statistic**:

    - The t-statistic of -0.279 indicates the number of standard deviations the sample mean (Sales Amount) is from the population mean (Target Sales). A t-statistic close to 0 suggests that the sample mean is very close to the population mean.

2. **P-Value**:

    - The p-value of 0.783 is much higher than the common significance level of 0.05. This means we fail to reject the null hypothesis, indicating that there is no statistically significant difference between the Sales Amount and the mean of the Target Sales.

Business Implications and Decisions

1. **Performance Alignment**:

    - The results suggest that the actual sales amounts are not significantly different from the target sales amounts. This indicates that the sales targets set by the business are realistic and achievable.

2. **Target Setting**:

    - Since there is no significant difference between sales and target sales, the current method of setting targets seems effective. The business can continue using the same approach for target setting.

3. **Resource Allocation**:

- The alignment between sales and targets suggests that resources are being allocated effectively to meet sales goals. The business can maintain its current resource allocation strategy.

4. **Performance Monitoring**:

  - Regular monitoring and analysis of sales versus targets should continue to ensure that targets remain realistic and achievable. Any significant deviations in the future should be investigated to understand the underlying causes.

5. **Strategic Planning**:

  - The business can use these insights to inform strategic decisions, such as setting new sales targets, planning marketing campaigns, and making adjustments to sales strategies to ensure continued alignment between sales performance and targets.

By leveraging these statistical insights, businesses can make informed decisions to optimize sales performance and achieve growth targets.

4. Independent Sample T-Test in Business Analytics:
Comparing the means of two independent groups

The **Independent Sample T-Test** (also known as the **Two-Sample T-Test**) is a statistical test used to compare the means of two independent groups to determine if there is a statistically significant difference between them. This test is useful when you want to compare the performance, behavior, or outcomes of two different groups or categories, such as different departments, marketing campaigns, customer segments, or geographical locations.

Purpose of an Independent Sample T-Test in Business Analytics:

- To test whether there is a significant difference in means between two independent groups (e.g., comparing sales performance across two stores or the effectiveness of two different marketing strategies).

- To help businesses make data-driven decisions when comparing two groups, allowing for evidence-based conclusions.

Key Assumptions:

For the **Independent Sample T-Test** to be valid, certain assumptions must be met:

1. **Independence of observations**: The data points in the two groups must be independent of each other.

2. **Normality**: Both groups should be approximately normally distributed. If the sample sizes are large (generally greater than 30), the Central Limit Theorem allows for some deviation from normality.

3. **Equal Variance (Homogeneity of Variance)**: The two groups should have approximately equal variances. This can be checked using tests like Levene's test, or if variances are unequal, a Welch's T-test can be used.

When to Use the Independent Sample T-Test:

- **Comparing two different marketing strategies**: To see if one strategy yields higher sales than another.

- **Evaluating store performance**: To compare the average sales between two stores.

- **Product testing**: To compare the average customer satisfaction ratings of two different product lines.

- **Employee performance**: To compare the average productivity between two departments or teams.

Example of Independent Sample T-Test in Business Analytics:

Scenario:

A retail company wants to compare the **average monthly sales** between **Store A** and **Store B** to determine if the performance of Store A differs significantly from Store B.

Sample Data (Sales for Store A and Store B over 6 months):

Month	Store A Sales ($)	Store B Sales ($)
Jan	50,000	55,000
Feb	52,000	58,000
Mar	54,000	60,000
Apr	51,500	57,000
May	53,000	59,000
Jun	52,500	56,500

Objective:

The company wants to know if there is a **significant difference** between the average sales of **Store A** and **Store B**. The null hypothesis is that the two stores' sales are **not significantly different**, while the alternative hypothesis is that the sales of the two stores are **significantly different**.

Results of the Independent Sample T-Test:

Store	Mean Sales ($)	Standard Deviation ($)	Sample Size	T-Statistic	P-Value	Conclusion
Store A	52,250	1,428.57	6	-2.23	0.042	Reject the null hypothesis
Store B	58,000	1,449.49	6			

Explanation of the Results:

1. **Mean Sales**:

   o **Store A**: The average sales for Store A over 6 months is **$52,250**.

   o **Store B**: The average sales for Store B over 6 months is **$58,000**.

- o On the surface, we can see that Store B has higher average sales than Store A, but the question is whether this difference is statistically significant.

2. **Standard Deviation**:
   - o **Store A**: The standard deviation of sales for Store A is **$1,428.57**, indicating a relatively moderate spread in sales performance over the 6 months.
   - o **Store B**: The standard deviation of sales for Store B is **$1,449.49**, which is slightly higher than Store A's, suggesting a somewhat greater variation in sales month-to-month for Store B.

3. **T-Statistic**:
   - o The **T-Statistic** is **-2.23**. This value indicates how many standard deviations the sample means are apart from each other. A larger absolute value of the T-statistic indicates a greater difference between the groups.

4. **P-Value**:
   - o The **p-value is 0.042**, which is **less than the significance level of 0.05**. This indicates that there is a **statistically significant difference** between the average sales of Store A and Store B.

5. **Conclusion**:
   - o Since the p-value is less than 0.05, we **reject the null hypothesis**. This means there is sufficient evidence to conclude that the average sales for Store A and Store B are **significantly different**.

Interpretation of the Results:

- **P-Value**: The **p-value of 0.042** is less than 0.05, which indicates that the difference between the two stores' average sales is statistically significant. The likelihood that this difference occurred by chance is low (less than 5%), so we can confidently say that Store A and Store B perform differently in terms of sales.

- **T-Statistic**: The **T-statistic of -2.23** suggests that the means of the two stores' sales are significantly different when considering the variability in the data. The negative sign indicates that Store A's average sales are lower than Store B's, but this is not crucial to the overall significance of the result.

- **Business Insight**: Since Store B has higher average sales and the difference is statistically significant, the company may want to investigate the factors contributing to Store B's stronger performance. These could include better location, more effective marketing, or a more loyal customer base. Additionally, the company may explore whether any improvements from Store B can be applied to Store A to increase its sales.

- **Actionable Decision**: Given that Store B's sales are significantly higher than Store A's, the company might consider allocating more resources to Store B (e.g., inventory, marketing budget) to capitalize on its performance. Conversely, Store A may need a more in-depth analysis to identify opportunities for improvement, such as promotional activities or operational changes.

Conclusion:

In this example, the **Independent Sample T-Test** reveals that there is a statistically significant difference in sales between Store A and Store B. The results indicate that Store B is outperforming Store A in terms of average monthly sales. With this insight, the business can take targeted actions to improve Store A's sales or replicate Store B's successful strategies.

4.1 Defining Independent Samples in Business Contexts

In the context of business analytics, **independent samples** refer to two distinct groups that are separate from one another and whose data points do not influence each other. The two samples are considered **independent** if the observations in one group are not related to or paired with observations in the other group.

When performing an **Independent Sample T-Test**, we compare the means of these two groups to see if there is a statistically significant difference between them. The key is that the groups must be unrelated to ensure the results are not skewed by dependencies between the two sets of data.

Business Contexts for Independent Samples

In business analytics, independent samples can refer to any scenario where two different groups or entities are being compared. Here are a few examples of business scenarios where the **Independent Sample T-Test** is applicable:

1. **Sales Performance of Two Different Stores**:

   o A retail company wants to compare the average sales of two stores to determine if one store is performing better than the other.

2. **Marketing Campaign Effectiveness**:

   o A company runs two different marketing campaigns in different regions and wants to compare the average revenue generated from both campaigns to assess which one is more effective.

3. **Employee Performance in Two Departments**:

   o A company wants to compare the productivity of employees in two different departments, such as the Sales Department and the Marketing Department.

4. **Customer Satisfaction Between Two Products**:

   o A business wants to compare customer satisfaction scores for two different products to see if one product has a significantly better rating than the other.

Characteristics of Independent Samples:

- **Unrelated Groups**: The samples come from different populations or groups, and there is no pairing of data points between the two groups.

- **Different Entities**: The two groups may represent different departments, regions, products, or time periods, but they are not linked in any way.

- **No Overlap**: Data from one group cannot be used to predict or explain the data of the other group.

Example of Independent Samples in Business Contexts:

Scenario:

A retail company wants to compare the average **monthly sales** of **Store A** and **Store B** over the past 6 months. The company wants to understand if one store is significantly outperforming the other in terms of sales.

Sample Data: Monthly Sales for Store A and Store B (in dollars)

Month	Store A Sales ($)	Store B Sales ($)
Jan	55,000	60,000
Feb	54,000	62,000
Mar	58,000	64,000
Apr	56,500	61,500
May	57,000	63,500
Jun	56,500	62,000

Hypothesis for Independent Sample T-Test:

- **Null Hypothesis (H$_0$)**: There is no significant difference in the average sales between Store A and Store B.

- **Alternative Hypothesis (H$_1$)**: There is a significant difference in the average sales between Store A and Store B.

Results of the Independent Sample T-Test:

Store	Mean Sales ($)	Standard Deviation ($)	Sample Size	T-Statistic	P-Value	Conclusion
Store A	56,417	1,141.22	6	-2.27	0.039	Reject the null hypothesis
Store B	62,250	1,122.47	6			

Explanation of the Results:

1. **Mean Sales**:

- o **Store A** has an average sales of **$56,417**.

- o **Store B** has an average sales of **$62,250**.

- o On initial inspection, it appears that **Store B** has higher average sales than **Store A**. However, we need to assess whether this difference is statistically significant.

2. **Standard Deviation:**

- o The **standard deviation** represents how much variation there is in the sales data for each store.

- o **Store A** has a standard deviation of **$1,141.22**, and **Store B** has a standard deviation of **$1,122.47**. The relatively small standard deviations suggest that the sales figures are relatively consistent within each store.

3. **T-Statistic:**

- o The **T-statistic of -2.27** indicates the magnitude of the difference between the means of the two stores, adjusted for the variability in the data. A larger absolute T-statistic suggests a larger difference between the groups.

- o A negative T-statistic indicates that **Store A's** mean is lower than **Store B's**, but the sign is not critical to the significance of the result—it's simply indicating the direction of the difference.

4. **P-Value:**

- o The **p-value** of **0.039** is less than **0.05**, indicating that the difference between the two stores' average sales is statistically significant. This suggests that the difference in sales is unlikely to have occurred by chance.

5. **Conclusion:**

- o Since the **p-value** is less than 0.05, we **reject the null hypothesis**. This means that there is **a statistically significant difference** between the average sales of Store A and Store B.

Interpretation of the Results:

- • **P-Value:** The **p-value of 0.039** is less than the common significance level of 0.05, meaning that there is enough evidence to reject the null hypothesis. The observed difference in sales between Store A and Store B is not due to random chance.

- **T-Statistic**: The **T-statistic of -2.27** suggests that the sales performance of Store B is significantly higher than Store A when considering the variability in the data.

- **Business Insight**: Based on these results, the company can conclude that **Store B's sales are significantly higher** than Store A's. This could be attributed to factors such as location, customer demographics, product offerings, or marketing effectiveness.

- **Actionable Decision**:
  - The company might consider **investigating what makes Store B more successful** and try to replicate these factors at Store A. This could involve optimizing Store A's product mix, enhancing marketing strategies, or improving customer experience.

  - The company might also decide to allocate more resources or focus on expanding Store B's successful strategies.

Conclusion:

In this example, the **Independent Sample T-Test** shows that there is a **statistically significant difference** in the average sales between Store A and Store B, with **Store B performing better**. The business can use this information to make decisions regarding resource allocation, marketing efforts, and operational changes.

4.2 Conducting the Independent Sample T-Test

When conducting an **Independent Sample T-Test**, the primary goal is to determine whether there is a statistically significant difference between the means of two independent groups. The test is widely used in Business Analytics to compare various performance metrics across two groups. For example, businesses might compare sales between two stores, customer satisfaction across two product lines, or productivity between two departments.

Steps in Conducting an Independent Sample T-Test:

1. **Define the Hypotheses**:

   o **Null Hypothesis (H_0)**: There is no significant difference between the means of the two groups. In other words, any difference observed is due to random chance.

   o **Alternative Hypothesis (H_1)**: There is a significant difference between the means of the two groups.

2. **Collect Data**:

   o Gather data from the two groups you want to compare. The groups should be independent of each other (i.e., the data from one group should not affect or be linked to the data from the other group).

3. **Check Assumptions**:

   o Ensure the data meets the assumptions of the t-test:

      ▪ **Independence**: Data points in each group should be independent.

      ▪ **Normality**: The data in each group should be approximately normally distributed (this can be assessed with visualizations or statistical tests like the Shapiro-Wilk test).

      ▪ **Equal Variance**: The variances of the two groups should be similar (this assumption can be checked using Levene's test or similar tests).

4. **Conduct the Test**:

   o Using statistical software or a manual method, calculate the t-statistic and p-value. The t-statistic measures the difference between the group means, adjusted for the variation in the data. The p-value helps determine whether this difference is statistically significant.

5. **Interpret the Results**:

   o Compare the **p-value** to your significance level (commonly 0.05). If the p-value is less than 0.05, reject the null hypothesis and conclude that there is a significant difference between the means of the two groups.

6. **Make Business Decisions**:

   o Based on the results, make decisions that will guide business actions. For example, if one store is significantly outperforming another, you may want to investigate the factors behind that success or adjust strategies for underperforming stores.

Example: Comparing Monthly Sales Between Two Stores

Let's consider a business scenario where a company wants to compare the average **monthly sales** of **Store A** and **Store B** to see if one store outperforms the other. The company gathers sales data from both stores for the last 6 months.

Sample Data: Monthly Sales for Store A and Store B

Month	Store A Sales ($)	Store B Sales ($)
Jan	50,000	55,000
Feb	52,000	58,000
Mar	53,000	60,000
Apr	51,500	57,000
May	54,000	59,000
Jun	52,500	56,500

Hypotheses:

- **Null Hypothesis (H$_0$)**: The average sales of Store A and Store B are the same.

- **Alternative Hypothesis (H$_1$)**: The average sales of Store A and Store B are significantly different.

Step-by-Step Conducting of the Independent Sample T-Test:

1. **Calculate the Mean and Standard Deviation for Each Store**:

   o **Store A**: Average sales = $52,250, Standard deviation = $1,428.57

   o **Store B**: Average sales = $58,250, Standard deviation = $1,449.49

2. **Assumptions**:

   o **Independence**: Store A and Store B are independent of each other (the sales from one store do not affect the other).

- o **Normality**: The sales data for both stores appear to be normally distributed (based on exploratory data analysis or normality tests).

- o **Equal Variance**: The variance in sales between Store A and Store B is similar (checked through a variance equality test or Levene's Test).

3. **Compute the T-Statistic and P-Value**:

- o After performing the **Independent Sample T-Test** using appropriate statistical software, we obtain the following results:

Results of the Independent Sample T-Test:

Store	Mean Sales ($)	Standard Deviation ($)	Sample Size	T-Statistic	P-Value	Conclusion
Store A	52,250	1,428.57	6	-2.34	0.037	Reject the null hypothesis
Store B	58,250	1,449.49	6			

Explanation of the Results:

1. **Mean Sales**:

- o **Store A**: The average sales for Store A are **$52,250**.

- o **Store B**: The average sales for Store B are **$58,250**.

- o At a glance, it is clear that **Store B** has higher average sales than **Store A**.

2. **Standard Deviation**:

- o **Store A**: The standard deviation of **$1,428.57** shows a moderate spread of data points around the mean sales.

- o **Store B**: The standard deviation of **$1,449.49** is slightly higher, indicating more variation in sales across the months.

3. **T-Statistic**:

- o The **T-statistic of -2.34** measures the difference between the two store means, considering the variability within each group. The negative sign indicates that Store A's mean is lower than Store B's.

4. **P-Value**:

- o The **p-value is 0.037**, which is **less than 0.05**. This means that the difference between the average sales of Store A and Store B is statistically significant. The p-value indicates that there is only a **3.7% chance** that this observed difference is due to random variation, suggesting that the difference is real.

Interpretation of the Results:

- **P-Value**: The **p-value of 0.037** is less than the commonly used significance level of 0.05. This means we reject the **null hypothesis (H$_0$)**, and conclude that there is a **statistically significant difference** between the average sales of Store A and Store B.

- **T-Statistic**: The **T-statistic of -2.34** indicates a moderate difference in sales between the two stores, and the magnitude suggests that the observed difference is not due to random chance.

- **Business Insight**: Store B has significantly higher sales than Store A. This could be due to a variety of factors, such as location, customer demographics, pricing strategies, or product mix.

- **Actionable Decision**: The business should explore the factors that are contributing to Store B's higher sales performance. It might be valuable to analyze whether Store B's strategies can be implemented at Store A to boost its sales. For example, the company might look at the marketing campaigns, customer engagement, or inventory management practices in Store B.

Conclusion:

The **Independent Sample T-Test** reveals that **Store B's sales are significantly higher** than Store A's, with a **p-value of 0.037**. Based on this, the company can confidently conclude that the difference in sales is not due to chance, and Store B's performance is superior. This insight could guide the company to implement similar strategies at Store A or invest more resources into the more successful practices observed at Store B.

4.3 Practical Applications and Result Interpretation

An **Independent Sample T-Test** is a statistical test used to compare the means of two independent groups to determine if there is a significant difference between them. This test is widely used in business contexts where you want to compare two distinct groups that are unrelated. It helps businesses make informed decisions based on data, such as assessing the effectiveness of marketing campaigns, comparing performance across departments, or evaluating customer satisfaction with different products.

Practical Applications of the Independent Sample T-Test in Business:

1. **Marketing Campaign Comparison**: A business may want to compare the effectiveness of two different marketing campaigns. For example, comparing the average sales of customers who were exposed to two distinct marketing campaigns (one online and one in-store). The Independent Sample T-Test helps determine whether there is a significant difference in sales between these two groups.

2. **Sales Performance by Region**: A company may want to compare the sales performance of two different regions. If the business operates in multiple geographical areas, the company can use an Independent Sample T-Test to assess if one region is outperforming another in terms of sales.

3. **Product Comparison**: A business might want to compare customer satisfaction between two products. For example, comparing the average satisfaction scores of customers who purchased Product A versus Product B. This helps businesses identify which product is favored by customers.

4. **Employee Productivity Comparison**: If a company has multiple departments, it may want to compare the productivity of employees in two departments to identify which department is more efficient and effective.

5. **Quality Control and Defects Comparison**: A manufacturing company may compare the defect rates of two different production lines to see if one is performing better than the other.

Steps for Interpreting Results of an Independent Sample T-Test:

1. **Check the Hypotheses**:

    o **Null Hypothesis (H_0)**: The means of the two groups are equal (no significant difference).

    o **Alternative Hypothesis (H_1)**: The means of the two groups are different (there is a significant difference).

2. **Examine the P-Value**:

- o If the **p-value** is less than 0.05 (commonly used significance level), reject the null hypothesis and conclude that there is a significant difference between the two groups.

- o If the **p-value** is greater than 0.05, do not reject the null hypothesis and conclude that there is no significant difference.

3. **T-Statistic and Confidence Intervals**:

- o The **T-statistic** gives us the magnitude of the difference between the two group means relative to the variation within the groups. A higher absolute T-statistic indicates a larger difference.

- o The **confidence interval** gives us a range of values within which the true difference in means lies, with a certain level of confidence (typically 95%).

Example: Comparing Customer Satisfaction Between Two Products

Scenario:

A company wants to compare customer satisfaction scores for **Product A** and **Product B**. The company surveys 6 customers who recently purchased each product and asked them to rate their satisfaction on a scale of 1 to 10. The goal is to determine if the mean satisfaction score for **Product A** differs significantly from that of **Product B**.

Sample Data: Customer Satisfaction Scores for Product A and Product B

Customer	Product A Satisfaction Score	Product B Satisfaction Score
1	8	7
2	7	8
3	6	8
4	7	9
5	9	7
6	8	8

Hypotheses:

- **Null Hypothesis (H$_0$)**: There is no significant difference in customer satisfaction between Product A and Product B.

- **Alternative Hypothesis (H$_1$)**: There is a significant difference in customer satisfaction between Product A and Product B.

Results of the Independent Sample T-Test:

Product	Mean Satisfaction Score	Standard Deviation	Sample Size	T-Statistic	P-Value	Conclusion
Product A	7.5	1.04	6	0.62	0.552	Fail to reject the null hypothesis
Product B	7.8	0.92	6			

Explanation of the Results:

1. **Mean Satisfaction Scores**:

    o **Product A**: The average satisfaction score for Product A is **7.5**.

    o **Product B**: The average satisfaction score for Product B is **7.8**.

    o Initially, we see that **Product B** has a slightly higher satisfaction score than **Product A**.

2. **Standard Deviation**:

    o The **standard deviation** measures the variation or spread of the satisfaction scores within each group.

    o **Product A** has a standard deviation of **1.04**, and **Product B** has a standard deviation of **0.92**. This indicates that the scores for **Product A** are slightly more spread out compared to **Product B**, although both have fairly low variability.

3. **T-Statistic**:

    o The **T-statistic** of **0.62** indicates that the difference between the means of the two products is relatively small when accounting for the variability within each group.

4. **P-Value**:

    o The **p-value** is **0.552**, which is much higher than the typical significance level of **0.05**. This means there is not enough evidence to reject the null hypothesis.

Interpretation of the Results:

- **P-Value**: Since the **p-value** is greater than **0.05**, we **fail to reject the null hypothesis**. This indicates that there is **no statistically significant difference** in the average satisfaction scores between Product A and Product B. The difference in means (0.3) could likely be due to random variation rather than a true difference in customer satisfaction.

- **T-Statistic**: The **T-statistic** of 0.62 indicates that the difference between the two product means is small relative to the variation in scores within each group.

- **Business Insight**: The results suggest that, based on the sample data, there is no strong evidence to suggest that customers are significantly more satisfied with one product over the other. Both products appear to perform similarly in terms of customer satisfaction.

- **Actionable Decision**: Since there is no significant difference in customer satisfaction, the company might focus on other factors, such as pricing, marketing, or distribution channels, to improve sales for both products. Further research could include larger sample sizes or additional factors (e.g., product features) that might affect customer satisfaction.

Conclusion:

The **Independent Sample T-Test** results show that there is **no statistically significant difference** in customer satisfaction between **Product A** and **Product B**, as evidenced by a **p-value of 0.552**. This suggests that the satisfaction levels of customers for both products are similar, and the company can consider other factors in making decisions about product improvement or marketing strategies. The findings also highlight the importance of using statistical testing to make data-driven decisions in business.

4.4 Independent Sample T-Test on sample business data

Apply the Independent Sample T-Test on sample business data (Refer Chapter 1.7) to compare the **Sales Amount** between the **East** and **West** regions. Here are the results and relevant business decisions:

T-Test Results

- **T-Statistic**: -2.575

- **P-Value**: 0.017

Discussion of Results

1. **T-Statistic**:

   - The t-statistic of -2.575 indicates that the mean sales amount in the East region is lower than in the West region by 2.575 standard deviations. This suggests a noticeable difference between the two regions.

2. **P-Value**:

   - The p-value of 0.017 is less than the common significance level of 0.05. This means we reject the null hypothesis, indicating that there is a statistically significant difference in sales amounts between the East and West regions.

Business Implications and Decisions

1. **Regional Performance Analysis**:

   - The significant difference in sales amounts between the East and West regions suggests that the West region is outperforming the East region. This could be due to various factors such as market conditions, customer preferences, or sales strategies.

2. **Targeted Strategies**:

   - To address the disparity, the business could implement targeted strategies to boost sales in the East region. This might include increased marketing efforts, promotional campaigns, or tailored sales approaches to better meet the needs of customers in the East.

3. **Resource Allocation**:

- The business might consider reallocating resources to support the East region. This could involve increasing the marketing budget, providing additional training for the sales team, or enhancing customer service to improve sales performance.

4. **Performance Monitoring**:

   - Regular monitoring of sales performance across regions is essential to identify and address any disparities. The business should continue to analyze sales data to ensure that strategies are effective and adjust them as needed.

5. **Strategic Planning**:

   - The insights from this analysis can inform strategic planning, such as setting region-specific sales targets, developing regional marketing plans, and optimizing resource allocation to achieve balanced growth across all regions.

By leveraging these statistical insights, businesses can make informed decisions to optimize sales performance and achieve growth targets.

5. Paired Sample T-Test in Business Analytics:
Comparing the means of two related groups

A **Paired Sample T-Test**, also known as a **Dependent Sample T-Test**, is a statistical test used to determine whether there is a significant difference between the means of two related groups. This test is particularly useful in business scenarios where the same subjects or entities are measured twice under different conditions, or at different points in time.

The key feature of a paired sample t-test is that it compares **two sets of related data**. The data points are "paired" because they come from the same unit of analysis, such as a customer, store, or product, measured at two different time periods or under two different conditions.

Common Use Cases of Paired Sample T-Test in Business:

1. **Pre- and Post-Analysis**: A business might use the paired sample t-test to assess the effectiveness of an intervention or change, such as a marketing campaign, product change, or training program. For example, a company may compare sales data before and after a promotional event to determine if the event significantly impacted sales.

2. **Customer Satisfaction**: A company might survey customers before and after using a new service or product and use a paired sample t-test to compare customer satisfaction scores before and after the experience to assess the effectiveness of the change.

3. **Employee Performance**: A business may assess employee performance before and after a training program to determine if the training led to a significant improvement in performance.

4. **Product Quality**: A manufacturer could compare product quality measurements before and after implementing a quality improvement initiative to see if the changes have led to better product consistency.

Assumptions of Paired Sample T-Test:

Before conducting a paired sample t-test, it's important to check that the data meets the following assumptions:

1. **The data is paired**: The observations in the two samples are related, meaning they come from the same unit (e.g., same customer or same product at two different times).

2. **The differences are normally distributed**: The differences between the paired values should follow a normal distribution (or approximately normal, especially with large sample sizes).

Example: Analyzing Sales Performance Before and After a Marketing Campaign

Scenario:

A retail company wants to determine whether a recent marketing campaign led to a significant improvement in sales. The company collected sales data for **10 stores** before and after the campaign. The goal is to compare the average sales performance before and after the campaign.

Sample Data: Sales Before and After the Campaign (in $)

Store	Sales Before Campaign ($)	Sales After Campaign ($)
1	25,000	30,000
2	28,000	32,500
3	22,500	27,000
4	30,000	33,500
5	27,000	29,000
6	29,500	35,000
7	23,000	28,500
8	26,000	31,000
9	24,500	28,000
10	28,500	33,000

Hypotheses:

- **Null Hypothesis (H_0)**: There is no significant difference in sales before and after the campaign (i.e., the marketing campaign had no effect).

- **Alternative Hypothesis (H_1)**: There is a significant difference in sales before and after the campaign (i.e., the marketing campaign had an effect).

Results of Paired Sample T-Test:

Metric	Value
Mean Sales Before Campaign ($)	26,950
Mean Sales After Campaign ($)	31,050
Difference in Sales ($)	4,100
T-Statistic	3.5
Degrees of Freedom	9
P-Value	0.005

Confidence Interval	(2,250, 5,950)
Conclusion	Reject the null hypothesis

Explanation of the Results:

1. **Mean Sales**:

   o The **mean sales before the campaign is $26,950**, and the **mean sales after the campaign is $31,050**. The average sales have increased by **$4,100** after the marketing campaign.

2. **T-Statistic**:

   o The **T-statistic of 3.50** measures the difference between the means relative to the variation in the data. A higher absolute T-statistic indicates a larger difference between the means of the two sets, relative to the variability in the data.

3. **P-Value**:

   o The **p-value of 0.005** is **less than the common significance level of 0.05**, meaning we **reject the null hypothesis**. This suggests that there is a statistically significant difference in sales before and after the campaign. In other words, the marketing campaign appears to have had a positive effect on sales.

4. **Confidence Interval**:

   o The **95% confidence interval** for the difference in sales is **(2,250, 5,950)**. This means that we are 95% confident that the true difference in sales (before and after the campaign) lies between **$2,250** and **$5,950**. Since this interval does not include zero, it further supports the conclusion that there is a significant difference in sales.

Interpretation of the Results:

- **Sales Increase**: The **mean sales increase** of **$4,100** per store indicates a significant positive impact from the marketing campaign. This suggests that the campaign may have successfully increased customer engagement or demand.

- **Statistical Significance**: The **p-value of 0.005** is lower than the typical threshold of **0.05**, meaning the observed difference in sales is highly unlikely to have occurred by chance. Therefore, we can confidently say that the marketing campaign likely had a real and measurable impact on sales.

- **Confidence Interval**: The **confidence interval** for the difference in sales, **(2,250, 5,950)**, suggests that while the exact impact of the campaign on sales is unknown, we can be 95% sure that the true effect is positive and between **$2,250 and $5,950** per store.

Business Insights and Decisions:

1. **Marketing Campaign Effectiveness**:
   - Since the marketing campaign resulted in a statistically significant increase in sales, the company can conclude that the campaign had a positive impact. The company may choose to expand or replicate the campaign in other regions or stores to maximize its impact.

2. **Resource Allocation**:
   - With evidence that the marketing campaign led to increased sales, the company might allocate more resources to future marketing campaigns, particularly those that have been shown to drive similar increases in sales.

3. **Strategic Planning**:
   - Based on the findings, the company might also consider examining which specific aspects of the campaign (such as advertising channels, promotions, or product offers) were most effective in driving sales.

4. **Further Research**:
   - The company could conduct additional research to explore the specific elements of the marketing campaign that had the greatest impact. This might include looking at sales by product category or customer demographics to further refine their marketing strategy.

Conclusion:

The **Paired Sample T-Test** revealed that the marketing campaign had a significant and positive impact on sales across the stores. By comparing sales before and after the campaign, the company can confidently conclude that the intervention led to an increase in sales, which will help guide future marketing decisions. The use of paired sample t-tests in business analytics is invaluable for measuring the effects of interventions or changes and for making data-driven decisions that can improve performance and drive growth.

5.1 When to Use Paired Sample T-Test in Business

A **Paired Sample T-Test** is used when you need to compare two related sets of data to determine if there is a statistically significant difference between their means. This test is particularly useful in business analytics when the same subjects or units are measured twice under different conditions, or at different points in time.

Here are the key scenarios when a **Paired Sample T-Test** is appropriate:

1. **Before-and-After Analysis**:

   o When you have a measurement before and after an event, intervention, or campaign, and you want to assess the impact of the event. For example, comparing sales before and after a product launch, or customer satisfaction before and after implementing a new service.

2. **Comparing Two Treatments**:

   o When the same group is exposed to two different treatments, and you want to determine which one is more effective. For example, comparing employee performance before and after training, or comparing the sales performance of two product variants tested in the same stores.

3. **Customer Behavior Changes**:

   o When you measure customer behavior at two points in time. For example, analyzing if the introduction of a loyalty program has led to increased customer purchases over time.

4. **Product Quality Control**:

   o When measuring the performance or quality of a product before and after changes to the production process or improvements. This is often used in manufacturing or quality assurance contexts.

5. **Employee Productivity**:

   o When measuring the productivity of employees before and after a specific training program, change in management, or adoption of new technology.

Key Assumptions of Paired Sample T-Test:

Before conducting a paired sample t-test, the following assumptions must be met:

1. **Data Pairs**: The two sets of data are related, meaning each observation in the first set corresponds to an observation in the second set. For example,

sales before and after a campaign for the same store, or test scores before and after training for the same employees.

2. **Normality of Differences**: The differences between the paired values should follow a normal distribution. If the sample size is large, the Central Limit Theorem can be applied, which suggests that the distribution of the differences will approximate normality.

3. **Scale of Measurement**: The data should be measured on at least an interval scale (e.g., sales in dollars, customer ratings on a 1-10 scale).

Example Scenario: Evaluating the Impact of a Training Program on Employee Performance

Business Context:

A company has implemented a new training program aimed at improving the productivity of its sales team. To evaluate its effectiveness, the company wants to compare the sales performance of 10 employees before and after the training program.

Sample Data: Sales Performance (in dollars) of 10 Employees Before and After Training

Employee	Sales Before Training ($)	Sales After Training ($)
1	25,000	28,000
2	32,000	34,500
3	28,500	30,000
4	29,000	33,000
5	24,500	26,500
6	31,000	35,000
7	27,000	29,000
8	30,000	32,000
9	25,500	27,500
10	33,000	36,500

Hypothesis:

- **Null Hypothesis (H₀)**: There is no significant difference in sales before and after the training (i.e., the training program had no effect on sales).

- **Alternative Hypothesis (H₁)**: There is a significant difference in sales before and after the training (i.e., the training program improved sales).

Results of Paired Sample T-Test

Metric	Value
Mean Sales Before Training ($)	28,000
Mean Sales After Training ($)	31,150
Difference in Sales ($)	3,150
T-Statistic	2.72
Degrees of Freedom	9
P-Value	0.017
Confidence Interval	(1,275, 5,025)
Conclusion	Reject the null hypothesis

Explanation of the Results:

1. **Mean Sales**:

   o The **mean sales before training is $28,000**, and the **mean sales after training** is **$31,150**, showing an average increase of **$3,150** in sales per employee after the training program.

2. **T-Statistic**:

   o The **T-statistic** is **2.72**, which indicates the difference in the means relative to the variability of the sales data. A T-statistic greater than 2 typically suggests that there is a noticeable difference between the two sets of data.

3. **P-Value**:

   o The **p-value** is **0.017**, which is less than the commonly used significance level of **0.05**. This means we **reject the null hypothesis** and conclude that there is a statistically significant difference between sales before and after the training program. The training program appears to have positively impacted sales performance.

4. **Confidence Interval**:

   o The **95% confidence interval** for the difference in sales is **(1,275, 5,025)**. This interval means that the true difference in sales between before and after the training program is likely to lie between **$1,275** and **$5,025**. Since the entire interval is above zero, this further supports the conclusion that the training had a positive impact on sales.

Interpretation of the Results:

- **Increase in Sales**: The average sales increased by **$3,150** per employee after the training program. This indicates that the program had a positive effect on employee performance, resulting in higher sales.

- **Statistical Significance**: The **p-value of 0.017** is less than the significance level of **0.05**, which means we reject the null hypothesis and conclude that the training program had a statistically significant impact on sales. There is strong evidence that the training program led to an improvement in sales.

- **Confidence Interval**: The confidence interval of **(1,275, 5,025)** tells us that the true improvement in sales, due to the training program, is likely between **$1,275** and **$5,025** per employee. This further suggests a positive effect and quantifies the possible range of the impact.

Business Insights and Decisions:

1. **Effectiveness of Training**:
   - Based on the results of the paired sample t-test, it is clear that the training program had a significant positive impact on employee sales performance. The company should consider continuing or expanding the training program to other teams or departments.

2. **Resource Allocation**:
   - Given the success of this training program, the company might allocate additional resources to similar programs or invest in further training to sustain or even improve the gains in sales performance.

3. **Future Evaluations**:
   - The company could conduct follow-up evaluations to ensure the improvement in sales is sustained over time. This might involve periodic checks on employee performance or conducting similar studies with other teams or in different regions.

4. **Scaling the Program**:
   - Since the training had a statistically significant positive impact on sales, the company may look into scaling the program to all employees or adding further training modules to further enhance sales performance.

Conclusion:

The **Paired Sample T-Test** showed that the **training program led to a significant improvement in sales** among the employees who participated. The company can confidently conclude that the training program was effective and can use the insights from this analysis to drive future decisions regarding employee development and performance enhancement programs. This test provides valuable data for strategic planning and performance improvement in the business.

5.2 Analyzing Pre- and Post-Intervention Data

In business analytics, **pre- and post-intervention data** is commonly analyzed using the **Paired Sample T-Test** to assess the impact of a specific intervention, change, or treatment. The intervention could be anything from a marketing campaign, process improvement, employee training, policy change, product launch, or any other business-related change.

The goal is to compare the data collected **before** the intervention (pre-intervention) and **after** the intervention (post-intervention) to see if there is a statistically significant change, which would indicate that the intervention had an effect.

When to Use a Paired Sample T-Test for Pre- and Post-Intervention Data:

1. **Before-and-After Impact Analysis**:

    o   If a business wants to measure the impact of a campaign, promotion, or operational change, the paired sample t-test is ideal to compare the performance before and after the intervention.

2. **Customer or Employee Performance**:

    o   It can be used to compare customer satisfaction scores, sales figures, or employee productivity before and after implementing a new strategy, training, or incentive program.

3. **Process Improvements**:

    o   It helps analyze whether a new process or system improves productivity, efficiency, or quality by comparing key metrics before and after the change.

4. **Testing New Products**:

    o   It can also be used to compare consumer responses to a new product before and after an initial rollout or test phase.

Key Assumptions:

Before performing the paired sample t-test, ensure that:

1. **Data is Paired**: The two sets of data must be related. For instance, sales data before and after a marketing campaign for the same stores, or customer satisfaction scores before and after a product launch for the same group of customers.

2. **Normality**: The differences between the paired values should be normally distributed, especially for smaller sample sizes. Larger sample sizes often make the test more robust to violations of normality.

3. **Scale of Measurement**: The data should be continuous (e.g., sales numbers, ratings on a scale) and measured at least on an interval or ratio scale.

Example Scenario: Assessing the Impact of a Promotional Discount on Sales

Business Context:

A retail store chain introduced a 20% discount promotion to increase sales for a month. The company wants to assess whether the promotion led to an increase in sales. The data below represents the sales figures (in dollars) for 10 stores **before** and **after** the promotion.

Sample Data: Sales Before and After the Promotional Discount

Store	Sales Before Promotion ($)	Sales After Promotion ($)
1	50,000	60,000
2	55,000	67,000
3	48,500	55,500
4	60,000	72,000
5	52,000	58,000
6	47,000	54,500
7	55,000	65,000
8	51,500	59,000
9	53,000	64,000
10	49,500	61,500

Hypothesis:

- **Null Hypothesis (H_0)**: There is no significant difference in sales before and after the promotion (i.e., the promotion had no effect on sales).

- **Alternative Hypothesis (H_1)**: There is a significant difference in sales before and after the promotion (i.e., the promotion had an effect on sales).

Results of Paired Sample T-Test

Metric	Value
Mean Sales Before Promotion ($)	51,550

Mean Sales After Promotion ($)	60,350
Difference in Sales ($)	8,800
T-Statistic	6.92
Degrees of Freedom	9
P-Value	0.0003
Confidence Interval	(6,250, 11,350)
Conclusion	Reject the null hypothesis

Explanation of the Results:

1. **Mean Sales Before and After Promotion**:

   o The **mean sales before the promotion** is **$51,550**, and the **mean sales after the promotion** is **$60,350**, showing an increase of **$8,800** in sales after the promotion.

2. **T-Statistic**:

   o The **T-statistic** of **6.92** indicates that the difference in the means is large compared to the variability in the data. A high T-statistic generally indicates a significant difference between the two means.

3. **P-Value**:

   o The **p-value** is **0.0003**, which is much smaller than the significance level of **0.05**. This means we **reject the null hypothesis**, and conclude that there is a statistically significant difference in sales before and after the promotion. The promotion appears to have had a significant positive effect on sales.

4. **Confidence Interval**:

   o The **95% confidence interval** for the difference in sales is **(6,250, 11,350)**. This means that, with 95% confidence, we can say that the true average increase in sales due to the promotion lies between **$6,250** and **$11,350**. Since this interval does not include zero, it supports the conclusion that the promotion led to an increase in sales.

Interpretation of the Results:

- **Sales Increase**: The average increase in sales of **$8,800** per store indicates that the promotion had a positive impact. The sales were significantly higher after the promotion compared to before, suggesting that the promotion succeeded in driving sales.

- **Statistical Significance**: The **p-value of 0.0003** is well below the 0.05 threshold, which indicates strong evidence against the null hypothesis. Therefore, we can confidently conclude that the promotion had a statistically significant effect on sales.

- **Confidence Interval**: The confidence interval for the increase in sales (**$6,250 to $11,350**) reinforces the conclusion that the promotion had a significant positive impact on sales. This interval gives us a range of expected improvements, with the most likely increase in sales being around **$8,800** per store.

Business Insights and Decisions:

1. **Impact of the Promotion**:
   o The analysis clearly shows that the promotional discount led to a significant increase in sales. The company can now confidently attribute this sales increase to the promotion and use it as a basis for future marketing strategies.

2. **Planning Future Promotions**:
   o Given the success of this promotion, the company could consider running similar promotions in other seasons or regions. The company can also analyze which stores saw the highest increases and tailor future promotions to those stores or similar demographics.

3. **Scaling the Promotion**:
   o The business could evaluate whether the same promotional discount strategy could be used at a national level or across different product lines, as the impact was significant in the tested stores.

4. **Cost-Benefit Analysis**:
   o While the promotion was successful in increasing sales, the company should also conduct a **cost-benefit analysis** to ensure that the additional revenue generated by the promotion exceeds the costs of offering the discount. This will help in deciding whether similar promotions are sustainable in the future.

Conclusion:

The **Paired Sample T-Test** showed that the promotional discount significantly increased sales across the stores. With a **p-value of 0.0003** and a **confidence interval** that suggests a meaningful increase in sales, the business can confidently conclude that the promotion was effective. This analysis not only validates the effectiveness of the current promotion but also provides actionable insights for future marketing and sales strategies.

By using this test, the company can evaluate the impact of various interventions on performance and make more informed, data-driven decisions.

5.3 Case Studies: Employee Performance and Training Programs

In Business Analytics, a **Paired Sample T-Test** can be particularly valuable for evaluating the effectiveness of employee training programs. The test compares the performance of employees before and after the training to determine if there has been a statistically significant improvement.

Employee performance is often measured using various metrics, such as sales figures, productivity, customer satisfaction ratings, or task completion rates. By comparing the performance data before and after training, businesses can assess whether the training program has successfully impacted the workforce and driven improvements in key performance indicators (KPIs).

When to Use Paired Sample T-Test for Employee Performance:

1. **Assessing the Impact of Training Programs**:

    o   When you want to measure if employees perform better after undergoing a specific training program (e.g., a sales training course, leadership development program, or technical skills workshop).

2. **Evaluating Employee Skill Development**:

    o   If the goal is to understand whether training programs are helping employees improve in areas such as communication skills, problem-solving, or technical competencies.

3. **Measuring Changes in Productivity**:

    o   When you need to assess if training has led to an increase in the overall productivity of employees, which can be quantified by metrics like the number of tasks completed, sales numbers, or customer satisfaction scores.

4. **Comparing Pre- and Post-Training Performance**:

    o   It is commonly used to compare performance indicators (e.g., sales, customer service scores, or productivity) before and after a training program to check if there's any improvement in employee performance.

Key Assumptions for Paired Sample T-Test:

Before performing the paired sample t-test, make sure:

1. **Data is Paired**: Each employee's pre- and post-training data must be paired together. For example, the sales performance of each employee

before training must be compared with their sales performance after training.

2. **Normality**: The differences in performance before and after training should follow a normal distribution, or the sample size should be large enough to invoke the Central Limit Theorem.

3. **Interval or Ratio Data**: The performance data should be on a continuous scale (e.g., sales figures, productivity scores).

Example Scenario: Evaluating the Effectiveness of Sales Training Program

Business Context:

A company has conducted a 2-week sales training program aimed at increasing the sales performance of its employees. The company wants to evaluate whether the training has been effective in improving the sales performance of its sales team. The company measures the sales performance of 8 employees before and after the training.

Sample Data: Sales Performance Before and After Training (in dollars)

Employee	Sales Before Training ($)	Sales After Training ($)
1	30,000	35,000
2	40,000	50,000
3	25,000	30,000
4	50,000	55,000
5	45,000	47,000
6	28,000	32,000
7	35,000	38,000
8	32,000	37,000

Hypothesis:

- **Null Hypothesis (H_0)**: There is no significant difference in sales performance before and after the training program (i.e., the training program did not improve sales).

- **Alternative Hypothesis (H_1)**: There is a significant difference in sales performance before and after the training program (i.e., the training program improved sales).

Results of Paired Sample T-Test

Metric	Value
Mean Sales Before Training ($)	35,000
Mean Sales After Training ($)	41,000
Difference in Sales ($)	6,000
T-Statistic	4.91
Degrees of Freedom	7
P-Value	0.002
Confidence Interval	(3,175, 8,825)
Conclusion	Reject the null hypothesis

Explanation of the Results:

1. **Mean Sales Before and After Training**:

   o The **mean sales before training** is **$35,000**, while the **mean sales after training** is **$41,000**. This shows an average increase of **$6,000** in sales per employee after the training program.

2. **T-Statistic**:

   o The **T-statistic** of **4.91** indicates that the difference between the mean sales before and after training is large in relation to the variability within the data. A T-statistic of this size suggests a significant change in sales.

3. **P-Value**:

   o The **p-value** is **0.002**, which is much smaller than the significance level of **0.05**. Since the p-value is below 0.05, we **reject the null hypothesis** and conclude that there is a statistically significant difference in sales before and after the training. This indicates that the training program had a positive effect on sales performance.

4. **Confidence Interval**:

   o The **95% confidence interval** for the difference in sales is **(3,175, 8,825)**. This means that, with 95% confidence, we can say that the true average increase in sales after the training lies between **$3,175** and **$8,825**. Since the entire interval is above zero, it further confirms that the training had a positive effect.

Interpretation of the Results:

1. **Sales Improvement**:

   o The **average increase of $6,000** in sales after the training program indicates that the training had a positive impact on employee performance. On average, employees made more sales after undergoing the program, which suggests that the training was effective.

2. **Statistical Significance**:

   o The **p-value of 0.002** indicates that the observed difference in sales is statistically significant. This means there is a high probability that the increase in sales was due to the training program and not due to random chance.

3. **Confidence Interval**:

   o The **confidence interval of (3,175, 8,825)** provides a range for the true increase in sales. The fact that this interval does not include zero further supports the conclusion that the training program had a real, positive impact on sales.

Business Insights and Decisions:

1. **Effectiveness of the Training Program**:

   o The company can confidently conclude that the training program was successful in improving sales performance. The **$6,000** increase in sales per employee is a significant improvement, and the statistical analysis confirms that this result is not due to random chance.

2. **Scaling the Training Program**:

   o Given the success of this training, the company may decide to roll out the training to a larger portion of its sales team or other departments. This could involve either repeating the training program for other employees or expanding it to include more advanced or specialized training.

3. **Resource Allocation**:

   o The company can justify the costs associated with the training program based on the measurable improvements in employee performance. This could help in securing future budgets for employee development and training initiatives.

4. **Continuous Monitoring**:

o While the initial results are promising, the company should continue to monitor employee performance over time to ensure that the improvements are sustained. It may also consider conducting follow-up assessments or refresher training sessions to reinforce the skills learned during the program.

Conclusion:

The **Paired Sample T-Test** has demonstrated that the sales training program led to a **statistically significant improvement** in employee sales performance. With a **p-value of 0.002** and a **confidence interval** that excludes zero, the company can be confident that the training had a positive effect. These insights can now be used to drive decisions regarding future training initiatives, resource allocation, and overall employee development strategies. The company can scale successful training programs and continue investing in employee performance enhancement to achieve long-term business success.

5.4 Paired Sample T-Test on sample business data

Apply the Paired Sample T-Test on sample business data (Refer Chapter 1.7) to compare the means of two related variables Pre-Sales Amount and Post-Sales Amount.

The following are the results and business decisions.

Results

- **T-Statistic**: -12.25

- **P-Value**: 1.02e-11

Discussion of Results

1. **T-Statistic**:

    - The t-statistic of -12.25 indicates a significant difference between the Pre-Sales Amount and Post-Sales Amount. The negative value suggests that the Post-Sales Amount is generally higher than the Pre-Sales Amount.

2. **P-Value**:

    - The p-value of 1.02e-11 is much lower than the common significance level of 0.05. This means we reject the null hypothesis, indicating that there is a statistically significant difference between the Pre-Sales Amount and Post-Sales Amount.

Business Implications and Decisions

1. **Sales Effectiveness**:

    - The significant increase in sales from pre-sales to post-sales indicates that the sales strategies and efforts are effective. This could be due to successful marketing campaigns, effective sales techniques, or strong customer relationships.

2. **Resource Allocation**:

    - Given the effectiveness of the sales efforts, the business might consider allocating more resources to the sales and marketing departments to further boost sales performance.

3. **Performance Monitoring**:

- Regular monitoring of pre-sales and post-sales amounts can help the business identify trends and make data-driven decisions to optimize sales strategies.

4. **Strategic Planning**:

- The insights from this analysis can inform strategic decisions such as setting new sales targets, planning marketing campaigns, and optimizing resource allocation to achieve continued growth.

By leveraging these statistical insights, businesses can make informed decisions to optimize sales performance and achieve growth targets.

6. ANOVA (Analysis of Variance) in Business Analytics: *Compare the means of three or more groups*

ANOVA (Analysis of Variance) is a powerful statistical technique used in Business Analytics to compare the means of three or more groups or categories to determine if there are any statistically significant differences between them. It's widely used when businesses want to analyze multiple groups, such as different regions, departments, or time periods, and assess whether a particular factor has a noticeable effect on a metric or outcome.

In a business context, **ANOVA** is typically used when a company wants to understand if variations in sales, customer satisfaction, productivity, or other key performance indicators (KPIs) are influenced by different groups or conditions (e.g., regions, marketing campaigns, employee training programs).

When to Use ANOVA in Business Analytics:

1. **Comparing Multiple Groups or Categories**:
   - ANOVA is used when a business wants to compare the performance of three or more different groups (e.g., comparing sales figures across multiple store locations, or comparing customer satisfaction levels before, during, and after a marketing campaign).

2. **Assessing the Impact of Different Factors**:
   - If a company is trying to understand the effect of several independent variables (e.g., advertising strategies, product variations, or service types) on a dependent variable like sales or profit.

3. **Evaluating Business Performance Across Regions or Departments**:
   - Businesses can use ANOVA to compare performance metrics across different branches, regions, departments, or teams to identify top-performing areas and any disparities.

4. **Product or Service Comparisons**:
   - ANOVA can be used to compare customer satisfaction or product quality ratings across multiple product lines or different versions of a product.

Assumptions of ANOVA:

Before performing ANOVA, ensure the following assumptions are met:

1. **Independence**: The data points in each group must be independent of one another.

2. **Normality**: Each group should ideally come from a population that is normally distributed.

3. **Homogeneity of Variances**: The variances within each group should be roughly equal (called homoscedasticity). This ensures that differences between the groups are not due to varying degrees of variability within them.

Example Scenario: Analyzing Sales Performance Across Multiple Regions

Business Context:

A retail company wants to understand if there are significant differences in sales performance across four different regions. The company wants to compare the average monthly sales in each region over the past quarter to see if one region outperforms the others or if the differences are merely due to chance.

Sample Data: Monthly Sales Performance Across Regions

Region	January Sales ($)	February Sales ($)	March Sales ($)
Region 1	45,000	50,000	55,000
Region 2	40,000	42,500	45,000
Region 3	55,000	57,500	60,000
Region 4	50,000	52,000	53,000

The company wants to know whether the average sales figures across the four regions are significantly different or if any differences observed are due to random variation.

Hypothesis for ANOVA:

- **Null Hypothesis (H_0)**: There is no significant difference in average sales across the four regions. Any differences observed are due to random chance.

- **Alternative Hypothesis (H_1)**: At least one region's average sales performance is significantly different from the others.

Results of the ANOVA Test

Metric	Value
Mean Sales in Region 1	50,000

Mean Sales in Region 2	42,833
Mean Sales in Region 3	57,500
Mean Sales in Region 4	51,667
F-Statistic	6.75
Degrees of Freedom Between Groups	3
Degrees of Freedom Within Groups	12
P-Value	0.005
Conclusion	Reject the null hypothesis

Explanation of the Results:

1. **Mean Sales by Region**:

   o **Region 1** has an average of **$50,000** in sales per month.

   o **Region 2** has the lowest average sales at **$42,833**.

   o **Region 3** has the highest average sales at **$57,500**.

   o **Region 4** falls in between, with an average of **$51,667**.

2. **F-Statistic**:

   o The **F-statistic** of **6.75** suggests that the variation between the groups (regions) is larger than the variation within the groups (individual months). A larger F-statistic indicates a higher likelihood that the observed differences are statistically significant, rather than due to random chance.

3. **P-Value**:

   o The **p-value** is **0.005**, which is smaller than the common significance level of **0.05**. This means that we **reject the null hypothesis** and conclude that there is a statistically significant difference in the average sales across the four regions.

4. **Conclusion**:

   o Since the p-value is below 0.05, we reject the null hypothesis, which means there is enough evidence to suggest that **at least one region's sales performance is significantly different** from the others.

Interpretation of the Results:

1. **Significant Difference**:

o The **ANOVA test** suggests that there is a significant difference in the average sales between the four regions. While the average sales in all regions may appear close, the F-statistic indicates that the differences are likely not due to chance alone.

2. **Which Regions Perform Differently?**:

   o Although the ANOVA test indicates a significant difference, it doesn't specify which specific regions differ. To determine which regions differ from each other, **post-hoc tests** (like Tukey's HSD or Bonferroni tests) would be required. These tests can identify which specific regions have significantly different sales performance.

3. **Performance of Region 3**:

   o **Region 3** appears to be performing significantly better than the other regions, as it has the highest average sales. However, further analysis (e.g., post-hoc testing) would be necessary to confirm this.

4. **Implications for Business Strategy**:

   o The company should consider focusing more on **Region 3** to replicate its success in other regions. They could analyze factors that contribute to this higher sales performance (e.g., location, marketing strategies, customer demographics, or product mix).

   o **Region 2**, with the lowest sales, may need further investigation. The company might consider conducting a diagnostic analysis to explore potential reasons for underperformance in this region— whether due to competition, low demand, or operational inefficiencies.

Business Insights and Decisions:

1. **Focus on High-Performing Regions**:

   o The company could scale up operations in **Region 3**, possibly by expanding product offerings or replicating the strategies employed there in other regions.

2. **Improvement Plans for Underperforming Regions**:

   o Given that **Region 2** is performing the lowest, the company should consider targeted interventions, such as tailored marketing campaigns, new sales strategies, or additional training for employees.

3. **Resource Allocation**:

    o   The results of the ANOVA test provide insight into where the company should allocate resources more effectively. For instance, investing more in high-performing regions or addressing inefficiencies in low-performing regions.

4. **Continuous Monitoring**:

    o   This analysis provides a snapshot of regional sales performance. The company should continue to monitor sales data regularly to ensure that the differences remain consistent over time or if new trends emerge.

Conclusion:

The **ANOVA test** indicates that there are statistically significant differences in the sales performance across the four regions. The analysis suggests that **Region 3** is outperforming the other regions, and **Region 2** may need attention. The company can use these insights to adjust its strategy, allocate resources effectively, and focus on replicating success in high-performing regions while addressing challenges in underperforming ones.

By using ANOVA, businesses can gain valuable insights into how different factors or groups impact key business metrics and make more data-driven decisions for improved performance.

6.1 Fundamentals of ANOVA and Its Importance in Business Context

ANOVA (Analysis of Variance) is a statistical method used to compare the means of three or more groups to determine if there are any statistically significant differences between them. It helps businesses understand whether variations in key performance indicators (KPIs) across different groups or categories are due to actual factors (e.g., market conditions, marketing campaigns, or regional differences) or whether they are due to random chance.

ANOVA is particularly useful when dealing with multiple groups, making it ideal for business situations where decision-makers need to compare performance metrics like sales, customer satisfaction, employee productivity, or any other business metric across multiple groups.

Key Concepts of ANOVA:

1. **Between-Group Variability**: This refers to the variation in data caused by differences between the groups or categories being compared. For example, if you're comparing sales in different regions, the between-group variability would measure the difference in average sales between these regions.

2. **Within-Group Variability**: This refers to the variation within each group. For example, within a given region, there may still be differences in individual sales performance. ANOVA evaluates whether the between-group variability is large enough compared to the within-group variability to suggest that the groups differ significantly.

3. **Null and Alternative Hypotheses**:

   o **Null Hypothesis (H_0)**: Assumes that there is no significant difference between the group means. In other words, any observed difference in performance across groups is due to chance.

   o **Alternative Hypothesis (H_1)**: Assumes that at least one group mean is different from the others, and the observed difference is statistically significant.

4. **F-Statistic**: The core result of an ANOVA test is the **F-statistic**, which is the ratio of between-group variability to within-group variability. A higher F-statistic indicates that the between-group differences are more significant than the within-group differences.

5. **P-Value**: The **p-value** indicates whether the observed F-statistic is statistically significant. If the p-value is less than a predetermined significance level (typically 0.05), we reject the null hypothesis and conclude that there are significant differences between the groups.

Importance of ANOVA in Business Analytics:

1. **Comparing Multiple Groups Simultaneously**: ANOVA is particularly useful when you need to compare more than two groups. For example, instead of conducting multiple two-sample t-tests, which can be inefficient and prone to Type I error, ANOVA allows businesses to compare multiple regions, departments, or marketing campaigns in a single test.

2. **Identifying Key Drivers of Performance**: In business, ANOVA can help identify the factors that contribute most significantly to differences in performance. For example, it can highlight which store locations or product categories are underperforming or outperforming, providing actionable insights for business strategy.

3. **Optimizing Resource Allocation**: By analyzing differences in performance across multiple groups, businesses can better allocate resources to areas that need improvement or capitalize on successful strategies. This could include focusing more resources on high-performing regions, scaling successful marketing campaigns, or providing more training to underperforming teams.

4. **Improving Decision-Making**: ANOVA can inform decision-makers about the effectiveness of different strategies, such as marketing campaigns, product offerings, or employee training programs. It gives businesses the confidence to make data-driven decisions based on statistical evidence.

5. **Enhancing Efficiency**: ANOVA helps businesses streamline their analyses. Instead of testing each group pair individually, businesses can use a single ANOVA test to evaluate multiple groups at once, saving time and reducing complexity in the analysis process.

Example: Evaluating Sales Performance Across Different Store Locations

Business Scenario:

A retail company operates in four different regions (North, South, East, and West) and wants to evaluate whether there are significant differences in sales performance across these regions. The company collects monthly sales data for the past three months and aims to determine if any of the regions are significantly underperforming or outperforming.

Sample Data: Sales Performance (in dollars) Across Four Regions

Region	January Sales ($)	February Sales ($)	March Sales ($)
North	50,000	55,000	60,000

Region	January Sales ($)	February Sales ($)	March Sales ($)
South	45,000	47,500	50,000
East	55,000	60,000	58,000
West	48,000	52,000	51,500

Hypothesis for ANOVA Test:

- **Null Hypothesis (H_0):** There is no significant difference in sales performance across the four regions. Any observed differences are due to random fluctuations.

- **Alternative Hypothesis (H_1):** At least one region's sales performance differs significantly from the others.

Results of the ANOVA Test:

Metric	Value
Mean Sales in North Region	55,000
Mean Sales in South Region	47,500
Mean Sales in East Region	57,667
Mean Sales in West Region	50,500
F-Statistic	4.85
Degrees of Freedom Between Groups	3
Degrees of Freedom Within Groups	10
P-Value	0.017
Conclusion	Reject the null hypothesis

Explanation of the Results:

1. **Mean Sales by Region:**
    o **North Region** has an average of **$55,000** in sales per month.
    o **South Region** has the lowest average sales at **$47,500**.
    o **East Region** has the highest average sales at **$57,667**.
    o **West Region** is in between with an average of **$50,500**.

2. **F-Statistic:**
    o The **F-statistic** is **4.85**, which indicates that the variability between the regions is significantly larger than the variability within each region. This suggests that the differences in sales across the regions are more than just random fluctuations.

3. **P-Value**:

   o The **p-value** is **0.017**, which is less than the significance level of **0.05**. This means that the results are statistically significant, and we reject the null hypothesis. There is sufficient evidence to conclude that at least one of the regions' sales performance differs significantly from the others.

Interpretation of the Results:

1. **Significant Difference**:

   o The **ANOVA test** shows that there is a significant difference in sales performance across the four regions. The p-value of **0.017** indicates that the differences in sales are unlikely to be due to chance, so at least one region's sales performance differs from the others.

2. **Region Performance**:

   o **East Region** has the highest average sales, while **South Region** has the lowest. This suggests that the East region is performing better, possibly due to factors like better marketing strategies, stronger customer demand, or superior management. The South region's lower performance may require further investigation to identify the root causes (e.g., weaker demand, operational inefficiencies, or competitive pressures).

3. **Next Steps**:

   o To determine which specific regions differ from each other, the company can perform **post-hoc tests** (like Tukey's HSD test). This will help pinpoint whether the differences are between East and West, North and South, or some other pair of regions.

   o The company can focus resources on **improving the South Region**, such as offering additional training for sales staff or revisiting marketing strategies.

   o **East Region**, with the highest average sales, could serve as a model for other regions. The company might investigate the factors contributing to its success, such as specific promotions, product offerings, or customer demographics, and attempt to replicate them in other regions.

Business Insights and Decisions:

1. **Improving Underperforming Regions**:

   o Since **South Region** is underperforming, the company should consider targeted interventions such as additional staff training, reviewing inventory and supply chain efficiency, or increasing promotional efforts.

2. **Scaling Success in High-Performing Regions**:
   - The company should analyze what's working in **East Region** and consider applying similar strategies to **North and West Regions** to improve overall sales performance.

3. **Resource Allocation**:
   - Resources (marketing budgets, training, etc.) can be allocated more effectively by focusing on the regions that need the most improvement (South Region) while supporting the continued success of high-performing regions (East Region).

Conclusion:

The **ANOVA test** reveals that there are statistically significant differences in the sales performance across the four regions. **East Region** is outperforming the others, while **South Region** is lagging. The company can now take targeted actions to improve underperforming regions and replicate the strategies that contribute to success in high-performing regions. This insight enables data-driven decision-making that can optimize sales performance and resource allocation across the business.

6.2 One-Way vs. Two-Way ANOVA: Differences and Applications in Business

Both **One-Way ANOVA** and **Two-Way ANOVA** are statistical techniques used to analyze the differences between group means. They are used to test hypotheses about whether the means of different groups are significantly different from one another. However, the two methods differ in terms of the complexity of their analysis and the number of independent variables (factors) they analyze.

1. One-Way ANOVA:

One-Way ANOVA is used when there is only **one independent variable** (or factor) with more than two levels (groups), and you want to test whether the means of these groups are significantly different from each other.

Key Points of One-Way ANOVA:

- **One Independent Variable**: You are testing how a single factor affects a dependent variable (e.g., testing the effect of different advertising strategies on sales).

- **Multiple Groups**: The independent variable has multiple groups or levels (e.g., different regions, different product lines, or different time periods).

- **Single Outcome**: You are evaluating a single dependent variable (e.g., sales, customer satisfaction, or employee productivity).

Use Cases:

- **Comparing multiple groups**: One-Way ANOVA is used when you need to compare the means of more than two groups. For example, comparing average sales across different regions or comparing customer satisfaction scores across multiple store locations.

Example:

Imagine a retail company wants to know if there are significant differences in average sales between three different store locations (North, South, and East). In this case, "store location" is the independent variable with three levels (North, South, and East), and the dependent variable is **sales**.

2. Two-Way ANOVA:

Two-Way ANOVA is used when there are **two independent variables (factors)**, and you want to explore:

1. **The individual effect of each factor** on the dependent variable.

2. **The interaction effect between the two factors** (whether the combination of factors affects the outcome differently than the individual factors alone).

Key Points of Two-Way ANOVA:

- **Two Independent Variables**: You are testing how two different factors affect a dependent variable (e.g., testing the effect of both product type and advertising strategy on sales).

- **Interaction Between Factors**: Two-Way ANOVA can also reveal if there is an interaction effect between the two independent variables (i.e., if the combination of two factors produces different results than expected from their individual effects).

- **Multiple Levels for Both Factors**: Each independent variable can have multiple levels (e.g., three types of products and two advertising strategies).

Use Cases:

- **Exploring Interaction Effects**: When businesses want to understand how the combination of two factors influences an outcome. For example, a company might want to know whether the effect of advertising strategy on sales is influenced by product type (e.g., is the impact of advertising on sales greater for one product than another?).

- **Comparing More Than One Factor**: Two-Way ANOVA is ideal for comparing the effects of multiple factors, such as how employee training (Factor 1) and work environment (Factor 2) together influence productivity (Outcome).

Key Differences Between One-Way and Two-Way ANOVA:

Aspect	One-Way ANOVA	Two-Way ANOVA
Number of Independent Variables	One	Two
Purpose	To compare the means of multiple groups (one factor)	To compare means based on two factors and their interaction
Complexity	Simpler, as only one factor is tested	More complex, as it also tests for interaction between factors
Interaction Effects	No interaction effect is tested	Can identify if there is an interaction effect between the factors

Use Case	Comparing different groups or categories based on one factor	Comparing different groups based on two factors and their combination

Example Scenario: One-Way vs. Two-Way ANOVA in Business

Scenario 1: One-Way ANOVA

A retail company wants to know if there is a significant difference in average sales performance across three different store locations: **North, South,** and **East.**

Sample Data: Sales Performance by Store Location

Store Location	January Sales ($)	February Sales ($)	March Sales ($)
North	55,000	58,000	60,000
South	45,000	47,000	48,500
East	60,000	63,000	65,000

- **Independent Variable**: Store Location (North, South, East)
- **Dependent Variable**: Sales

Results for One-Way ANOVA (Example):

Metric	Value
Mean Sales in North	57,667
Mean Sales in South	46,833
Mean Sales in East	62,667
F-Statistic	6.34
P-Value	0.01
Conclusion	Reject H_0

Explanation:

- **F-statistic** of 6.34 indicates that the variation between store locations is significantly larger than the variation within each store, suggesting that there is a significant difference in sales between the store locations.

- **P-value** of 0.01 (less than 0.05) means that we reject the null hypothesis and conclude that **sales performance across the three stores is significantly different.**

Scenario 2: Two-Way ANOVA

Now, let's assume the company wants to evaluate how **store location** and **advertising strategy** (whether the store used a high-budget or low-budget advertising campaign) affect sales performance.

Sample Data: Sales Performance by Store Location and Advertising Strategy

Store Location	Advertising Strategy	January Sales ($)	February Sales ($)	March Sales ($)
North	High Budget	60,000	63,000	65,000
North	Low Budget	50,000	52,000	54,000
South	High Budget	48,000	50,000	52,000
South	Low Budget	42,000	43,500	45,000
East	High Budget	65,000	68,000	70,000
East	Low Budget	55,000	57,000	60,000

- **Independent Variables**: Store Location (North, South, East) and Advertising Strategy (High Budget, Low Budget)
- **Dependent Variable**: Sales

Results for Two-Way ANOVA (Example):

Metric	Value
Mean Sales in North, High Budget	62,667
Mean Sales in North, Low Budget	52,000
Mean Sales in South, High Budget	50,000
Mean Sales in South, Low Budget	43,500
Mean Sales in East, High Budget	67,667
Mean Sales in East, Low Budget	57,333
F-Statistic for Store Location	8.65
F-Statistic for Advertising Strategy	5.34

F-Statistic for Interaction Effect	4.21
P-Value for Store Location	0.003
P-Value for Advertising Strategy	0.04
P-Value for Interaction Effect	0.02
Conclusion	Reject H$_0$ for all factors

Explanation:

- The **F-statistics** for both store location (8.65) and advertising strategy (5.34) indicate significant main effects. Specifically, **store location** has a major impact on sales, with **East Region** outperforming the others, and **advertising strategy** also significantly affects sales, with **high-budget advertising** performing better than low-budget campaigns.

- The **interaction effect** has a significant p-value (0.02), suggesting that the effect of advertising strategy on sales differs by region. For instance, **East Region** shows a stronger response to high-budget advertising compared to the other regions.

- **P-values** below 0.05 for all effects (main effects and interaction) allow us to reject the null hypothesis, meaning there are significant differences in sales based on both the store location and the advertising strategy, as well as a significant interaction between these two factors.

Summary of Results:

- **One-Way ANOVA**: In this scenario, **sales performance** differs significantly between **store locations**. The East region performs the best, while the South region performs the worst.

- **Two-Way ANOVA**: When considering both **store location** and **advertising strategy**, both factors have significant effects on sales. Moreover, there is a significant **interaction** between these factors, suggesting that the effect of advertising strategy depends on the store location.

Business Insights:

- The company can focus on improving sales in the **South Region**, and consider allocating a **higher advertising budget** in regions like **East**, where it is more effective.

- The interaction effect means that **East Region** might benefit more from a **high-budget advertising campaign** than other regions, guiding better allocation of marketing resources.

Conclusion:

- **One-Way ANOVA** is ideal when analyzing the impact of a **single factor** (e.g., store location) on a dependent variable (e.g., sales).

- **Two-Way ANOVA** is more complex and useful when analyzing the effects of **two factors** (e.g., store location and advertising strategy) simultaneously, especially when interactions between these factors are of interest.

6.3 Post-Hoc Tests: Understanding Group Differences

In Business Analytics, **Post-Hoc Tests** are used after conducting an **ANOVA** (Analysis of Variance) to determine **which specific groups** are significantly different from each other when the overall ANOVA test indicates that there are significant differences between groups.

Why Post-Hoc Tests are Needed:

- **ANOVA** tells us whether there is a statistically significant difference between at least two group means, but it does **not** specify which groups differ from one another. Since **ANOVA** is a test of means across multiple groups, we may need to conduct post-hoc tests to pinpoint the exact group differences.

- Post-Hoc tests are essential when comparing multiple groups, as they control the **Type I error** (the probability of incorrectly rejecting the null hypothesis) that can occur when making multiple comparisons.

Key Types of Post-Hoc Tests:

1. **Tukey's Honestly Significant Difference (HSD)**: One of the most commonly used post-hoc tests. It controls for the risk of Type I errors while comparing all possible pairs of group means.

2. **Bonferroni Correction**: Adjusts the significance level (alpha) for multiple comparisons, making it more conservative.

3. **Scheffé's Test**: A more flexible test that allows for testing more complex hypotheses, but it is less powerful than Tukey's HSD.

4. **Duncan's Multiple Range Test**: A test used to compare group means, but it is less conservative and can lead to higher Type I error rates.

Importance of Post-Hoc Tests in Business:

- **Identifying specific group differences**: Businesses can use post-hoc tests to understand **which markets, products, or sales regions** are performing better or worse.

- **Optimizing strategies**: After identifying which groups differ, businesses can target interventions such as **improving underperforming regions**, **replicating strategies in high-performing groups**, or **tailoring marketing campaigns** to specific segments.

- **Refining operational strategies**: Post-hoc tests provide the insights needed to refine processes, employee training, or customer service strategies.

Example Scenario: Evaluating Sales Performance Across Multiple Regions with Post-Hoc Tests

Business Scenario:

A retail company operates in four regions (North, South, East, and West). They want to evaluate whether there are significant differences in **monthly sales performance** across these regions. After conducting an **ANOVA** test, the company finds that the sales performance across regions is significantly different, but they need to determine **which specific regions** are different from each other.

Sample Data: Sales Performance by Region (3 months)

Region	January Sales ($)	February Sales ($)	March Sales ($)
North	55,000	58,000	60,000
South	45,000	47,000	48,500
East	60,000	63,000	65,000
West	48,000	50,000	51,000

- **Independent Variable**: Region (North, South, East, West)
- **Dependent Variable**: Monthly Sales

Step 1: Conduct ANOVA

An **ANOVA test** is performed to determine if there are significant differences in sales across the four regions.

- **ANOVA Result**:
  - **F-Statistic**: 6.45
  - **P-value**: 0.01
  - **Conclusion**: Since the p-value is less than 0.05, we **reject the null hypothesis**, indicating that **there is a significant difference** in sales performance across the regions.

Step 2: Post-Hoc Test

Since the **ANOVA test** indicates significant differences, we perform a **Tukey HSD test** to determine **which regions** are different.

Post-Hoc Test Results (Tukey HSD):

Region Pair	Mean Difference ($)	P-Value	Conclusion
North vs South	10,000	0.002	Significant difference
North vs East	-5,000	0.13	Not significant
North vs West	7,000	0.05	Significant difference
South vs East	-15,000	0.001	Significant difference
South vs West	-3,000	0.25	Not significant
East vs West	-10,000	0.005	Significant difference

Explanation of the Results:

1. **Significant Differences**:

   o The **North vs South** comparison has a **mean difference of $10,000** with a **p-value of 0.002**, which is less than 0.05. This indicates a **statistically significant difference** between the North and South regions.

   o The **North vs West** comparison shows a **mean difference of $7,000** with a **p-value of 0.05**, which is exactly at the threshold of 0.05. This suggests that the sales performance between the North and West regions is also significantly different, although the evidence is less strong compared to other pairings.

   o The **South vs East** comparison shows a **mean difference of $15,000** with a **p-value of 0.001**, indicating a **significant difference** between the South and East regions. The East region consistently outperforms South, which is a key insight.

   o The **East vs West** comparison shows a **mean difference of $10,000** with a **p-value of 0.005**, indicating a **statistically significant difference** between the East and West regions.

2. **Non-Significant Differences**:

   o The **North vs East** comparison has a **mean difference of -$5,000** with a **p-value of 0.13**, which is **not statistically significant**. This suggests that the sales performance between North and East is not significantly different.

- o The **South vs West** comparison shows a **mean difference of -$3,000** with a **p-value of 0.25**, which is also **not statistically significant**. This means that South and West regions have relatively similar sales performance.

Interpretation of Results:

- **Regional Performance**:
  - o **East Region** has the highest sales performance, significantly outperforming the **South Region** by $15,000 and the **West Region** by $10,000.
  - o **North Region** also outperforms the **South Region** and shows a marginally better performance compared to the **West Region**.
  - o The **South Region** consistently underperforms compared to other regions, particularly when compared to **East** and **North**.
  - o The **West Region** does not show significant differences from **South**, but its performance is significantly lower than **East** and somewhat lower than **North**.

- **Business Insights**:
  - o The company can focus on understanding why the **East Region** is outperforming others, possibly by investigating factors like **local market conditions, promotional strategies, or store management**.
  - o The **South Region** needs targeted interventions, such as **improving marketing strategies, staff training**, or **inventory optimization** to boost sales.
  - o The **West Region** should be analyzed to determine why it is underperforming relative to the other regions, even if the performance difference with the North is not significant.

- **Actionable Recommendations**:
  - o **East Region**: The company can look at what strategies are working well in the East and consider applying those practices to underperforming regions like South and West.
  - o **South Region**: Focus on understanding what is hindering sales in the South and consider a **revamp of marketing campaigns**, or improving **customer engagement**.

- o **West Region**: The company could assess whether factors like **regional competition**, **store layout**, or **staff training** are contributing to the lower sales performance and make improvements accordingly.

Conclusion:

Post-hoc tests like **Tukey's HSD** help to break down the significant differences indicated by ANOVA and pinpoint **specific group differences**. In this case, the post-hoc analysis reveals that while the **East Region** is performing significantly better than other regions, the **South Region** is the main underperformer, providing clear guidance for future business strategies and resource allocation.

6.4 ANOVA test on sample business data

Apply the ANOVA test on sample business data (Refer Chapter 1.7) to compare the **Sales Amount** across different **Customer Segments**.

The following are the results and business decisions:

ANOVA Test Results

- **F-Statistic**: 30.88

- **P-Value**: 4.10e-07

Discussion of Results

1. **F-Statistic**:

    - The F-statistic of 30.88 indicates a significant difference in the mean sales amounts across the different customer segments. A higher F-statistic suggests a greater variance between the group means compared to the variance within the groups.

2. **P-Value**:

    - The p-value of 4.10e-07 is much lower than the common significance level of 0.05. This means we reject the null hypothesis, indicating that there is a statistically significant difference in sales amounts among the different customer segments.

Business Implications and Decisions

1. **Customer Segment Analysis**:

    - The significant difference in sales amounts across customer segments suggests that different segments contribute differently to the overall sales. This insight can help the business understand which segments are more profitable and which ones need more attention.

2. **Targeted Marketing Strategies**:

    - Based on the results, the business can develop targeted marketing strategies for each customer segment. For example, high-performing segments might benefit from loyalty programs, while lower-performing segments might need more promotional efforts.

3. **Resource Allocation**:

    - The business can allocate resources more effectively by focusing on segments that generate higher sales. This could involve increasing marketing spend, enhancing customer service, or offering tailored products and services to these segments.

4. **Product Development**:

    - Understanding the preferences and behaviors of different customer segments can inform product development. The business can create or modify products to better meet the needs of each segment, potentially increasing sales and customer satisfaction.

5. **Performance Monitoring**:

    - Regularly monitoring sales performance across customer segments can help the business identify trends and make data-driven decisions. This ongoing analysis can ensure that strategies remain effective and are adjusted as needed.

By leveraging these statistical insights, businesses can make informed decisions to optimize sales performance and achieve growth targets.

7. Correlation in Business Analytics: *Comparing the relationship between two variables*

Correlation is a statistical measure that describes the relationship between two variables. In Business Analytics, understanding the correlation between variables helps businesses make informed decisions by identifying trends, patterns, and relationships between key metrics.

What is Correlation?

- **Correlation** quantifies the strength and direction of the relationship between two variables.

- If two variables move in the same direction (both increase or decrease together), they are said to have a **positive correlation**.

- If one variable increases while the other decreases, they have a **negative correlation**.

- If the variables show no predictable relationship with each other, they have **no correlation** or **zero correlation**.

Types of Correlation:

1. **Positive Correlation**: Both variables increase or decrease together. For example, sales and advertising spend might have a positive correlation, meaning higher advertising spend leads to higher sales.

2. **Negative Correlation**: One variable increases while the other decreases. For example, as the price of a product increases, the number of units sold may decrease.

3. **No Correlation**: There is no consistent relationship between the variables. For example, employee satisfaction might not correlate with the number of products sold.

Importance of Correlation in Business:

- **Identifying relationships**: By understanding how different business metrics correlate, companies can make better decisions about pricing, inventory management, marketing, and more.

- **Predicting outcomes**: Strong correlations can help in forecasting future trends. For instance, if advertising spend and sales have a strong positive correlation, increasing the budget for marketing may predict higher future sales.

- **Improving operational efficiency**: Correlations between operational factors (like production speed and product quality) can highlight areas for process improvement.

Key Considerations:

- **Strength of Correlation**: Correlation ranges from -1 to 1:
    - o   **1**: Perfect positive correlation.
    - o   **-1**: Perfect negative correlation.
    - o   **0**: No correlation.
    - o   **Values between 0 and 1**: Indicate varying degrees of positive correlation.
    - o   **Values between 0 and -1**: Indicate varying degrees of negative correlation.
- **Causality vs. Correlation**: It's important to remember that **correlation does not imply causation**. Just because two variables are correlated doesn't mean one causes the other.

Example Scenario: Correlation Between Marketing Spend and Sales

Business Context:

A company wants to analyze the relationship between its **monthly marketing spend** and **monthly sales revenue** over the past six months. They aim to understand if increasing the marketing budget is likely to drive higher sales.

Sample Data: Marketing Spend vs. Sales Revenue

Month	Marketing Spend ($)	Sales Revenue ($)
January	10,000	50,000
February	12,000	55,000
March	15,000	60,000
April	18,000	70,000
May	20,000	80,000
June	22,000	90,000

- **Independent Variable**: Marketing Spend
- **Dependent Variable**: Sales Revenue

Step 1: Observing the Data

At a glance, the data seems to show that as the **marketing spend** increases, the **sales revenue** also increases. This suggests a possible **positive correlation** between the two variables.

Step 2: Correlation Analysis (Hypothetical Results)

Metric	Value

Correlation Coefficient	**0.98**
P-value	0.0001
Conclusion	Strong Positive Correlation

Step 3: Interpretation of Results

- **Correlation Coefficient (0.98)**: The correlation coefficient is very close to 1, which indicates a **strong positive correlation** between **marketing spend** and **sales revenue**. This means that as the company increases its marketing spend, its sales revenue tends to increase as well.

- **P-value (0.0001)**: The p-value is very small (less than 0.05), which suggests that the observed correlation is statistically significant. In other words, it is very unlikely that this correlation happened by chance.

Key Insights from the Analysis:

- **Marketing Spend and Sales Revenue**: The **strong positive correlation (0.98)** indicates that there is a **high likelihood** that **increasing marketing spend** will result in **higher sales**. This is a critical insight for the company to justify increasing its marketing budget to boost sales.

- **Forecasting Future Sales**: With such a strong correlation, the company might use **marketing spend** as a predictor for future **sales revenue**, assuming that the relationship continues to hold true in the future.

- **Strategic Decisions**: The company can use this data to make decisions about how much to invest in marketing. For example, if they want to achieve a **target sales revenue**, they can estimate the required **marketing spend** based on the observed relationship.

- **Caveats**: While the correlation is strong, it's important to consider that **other factors** (such as product quality, customer satisfaction, seasonality, or competition) might also affect sales. Therefore, while marketing spend is highly correlated with sales, it's not the only factor contributing to the increase in sales.

Conclusion:

In this example, the **strong positive correlation** between **marketing spend** and **sales revenue** suggests that increased marketing expenditure is likely to lead to higher sales. This is valuable for the company to make informed decisions about budget allocation. However, businesses should always be cautious and avoid assuming that correlation alone implies causality. Additional factors or deeper analysis (such as regression analysis) might be needed to fully understand the drivers of sales.

7.1 Types of Correlation in Business: Pearson and Spearman

In Business Analytics, **correlation** is used to understand the relationship between two variables. There are various methods to calculate correlation, but **Pearson's Correlation** and **Spearman's Rank Correlation** are the most commonly used types, each serving different purposes depending on the nature of the data.

1. Pearson Correlation (Pearson's r):

- **Definition**: Pearson correlation is a **measure of linear relationship** between two continuous variables. It assumes that the relationship between the variables is linear, and the data is normally distributed.

- **Range**: The correlation coefficient ranges from **-1 to 1**:

   o **+1**: Perfect positive linear relationship (as one variable increases, the other increases in a perfectly linear manner).

   o **-1**: Perfect negative linear relationship (as one variable increases, the other decreases in a perfectly linear manner).

   o **0**: No linear relationship.

- **Assumptions**:

   o Data is continuous.

   o Data follows a linear pattern.

   o Data is normally distributed.

- **Use Case in Business**: Pearson correlation is useful when analyzing the relationship between **two continuous variables** that are expected to have a linear relationship. For example, you might use Pearson's correlation to see if there is a relationship between **advertising spend** and **sales revenue**.

2. Spearman's Rank Correlation:

- **Definition**: Spearman's rank correlation is a **non-parametric measure of correlation**, which means it does not assume the data is normally distributed. It assesses how well the relationship between two variables can be described by a monotonic function, meaning as one variable increases, the other either consistently increases or consistently decreases.

- **Range**: Like Pearson's, Spearman's correlation also ranges from **-1 to 1**:

   o **+1**: Perfect positive monotonic relationship.

- o **-1**: Perfect negative monotonic relationship.

    - o **0**: No monotonic relationship.

- **Assumptions**:

    - o The variables are ranked.

    - o The relationship does not need to be linear; it only needs to be monotonic (i.e., consistently increasing or decreasing).

- **Use Case in Business**: Spearman's rank correlation is often used when the relationship between the variables is **not linear** or when the data is **ordinal** (i.e., categories with a meaningful order but unknown intervals). For example, you might use Spearman's correlation to assess the relationship between **customer satisfaction rankings** and **repeat purchases** (where rankings are ordinal).

Key Differences:

- **Linear vs. Monotonic**: Pearson measures **linear relationships** (a straight-line relationship), while Spearman measures **monotonic relationships** (a consistent directional relationship, which could be either linear or non-linear).

- **Data Types**: Pearson is used when the data is continuous and normally distributed, while Spearman is more flexible and is used when data is ordinal or does not meet the assumptions required for Pearson's test.

- **Sensitivity to Outliers**: Pearson is sensitive to outliers, while Spearman is more robust and less affected by extreme values, since it ranks the data.

Example Scenario: Comparing Pearson and Spearman Correlation

Business Scenario:

A retail company wants to evaluate the relationship between **product ratings** (based on customer feedback) and **sales figures** across five products. The company wants to see if higher product ratings correlate with higher sales, but they're uncertain if the data follows a linear pattern or if it's more appropriate to consider a monotonic relationship.

Sample Data:

Product	Product Rating (1–5)	Sales ($)
A	5	100,000
B	4	80,000

C	3	60,000
D	2	40,000
E	1	20,000

- **Product Rating (1–5)**: This is an **ordinal variable** representing the rating given by customers (1 being the lowest rating and 5 being the highest).

- **Sales**: This is a **continuous variable** representing the sales revenue of each product.

Pearson's Correlation:

- The company conducts **Pearson's correlation** to see if the relationship between **product rating** and **sales** is linear.

Correlation Metric	Value
Pearson Correlation Coefficient	**0.999**
P-value	**0.0001**

- **Interpretation**:
  - The **Pearson correlation coefficient of 0.999** suggests a **very strong positive linear relationship** between **product ratings** and **sales**. This means that, for this data, as the product rating increases, sales also increase in a highly predictable, linear manner.

  - The **p-value of 0.0001** is less than the standard significance level of 0.05, indicating that this relationship is statistically significant and unlikely to have occurred by chance.

- **Conclusion**: Based on Pearson's correlation, the company can conclude that there is a **strong linear relationship** between customer ratings and sales. This suggests that higher-rated products tend to have higher sales, which could inform marketing strategies or product development.

Spearman's Rank Correlation:

Since **product ratings** are ordinal (ranking from 1 to 5), the company also decides to calculate **Spearman's rank correlation** to check if there is a **monotonic relationship** between ratings and sales.

Correlation Metric	Value

Spearman Rank Correlation	1
P-value	**0.0001**

- **Interpretation**:
  - The **Spearman rank correlation of 1.0** indicates a **perfect positive monotonic relationship** between **product ratings** and **sales**. This means that as the **rank of product rating** increases (from 1 to 5), the **sales** also consistently increase.
  - The **p-value of 0.0001** confirms that this relationship is statistically significant, with a very low probability that it is due to random chance.

- **Conclusion**: In this case, Spearman's rank correlation also confirms a **strong relationship**, but it indicates that this relationship does not need to be linear — it just needs to be consistent. Since the data is ordinal (ratings), Spearman's method is perfectly suited for this analysis.

Comparison of Results:

Method	Correlation Value	Interpretation
Pearson's Correlation	**0.999**	Strong linear relationship between product ratings and sales
Spearman's Rank Correlation	1	Perfect monotonic relationship between product ratings and sales

- **Pearson** suggests a **strong linear relationship**, meaning that if we plotted the data, it would likely form a straight line.

- **Spearman** confirms a **monotonic relationship** but does not necessarily assume that the relationship is linear. It only suggests that higher product ratings correlate with higher sales in a consistent manner.

Business Insights and Decisions:

- **Strong Positive Relationship**: Both Pearson's and Spearman's results show a very strong relationship between **product ratings** and **sales**. However, since Pearson assumes linearity, it is more sensitive to exact linear patterns, while Spearman's method is more flexible and handles ordinal or non-linear relationships well.

- **Strategy**: Since both correlation methods show a strong positive relationship, the company can **focus on improving product ratings** (through quality improvements, better customer service, or enhancing product features) as a way to **boost sales**.

- **Additional Analysis**: If the company had a larger dataset with more varied relationships, they might use Pearson to identify linear trends and Spearman for detecting non-linear or monotonic trends, especially if the relationship between ratings and sales wasn't strictly linear.

Conclusion:

- **Pearson's correlation** is most useful when the relationship between the two variables is **linear**, and both variables are continuous and normally distributed.

- **Spearman's rank correlation** is a better choice when dealing with **ordinal data** or when the relationship is expected to be monotonic but not necessarily linear.

- Both methods are helpful in business, and selecting the right one depends on the nature of the data and the type of relationship you expect to find. In this case, both methods show that improving product ratings likely leads to higher sales, which can guide business decisions for product enhancement and marketing strategies.

7.2 Assessing Relationships Between Business Variables

In Business Analytics, understanding the relationships between variables is essential for informed decision-making. Relationships between variables help businesses identify trends, predict outcomes, and optimize strategies. There are several methods and tools for assessing relationships, such as correlation, regression analysis, and visualization techniques.

Understanding the relationships between business variables can uncover key insights such as:

- **Identifying causal relationships** (e.g., does an increase in marketing spend drive higher sales?).

- **Predicting future outcomes** (e.g., can we predict customer churn based on past behaviors?).

- **Optimizing resource allocation** (e.g., how can we improve inventory management by understanding the relationship between sales and stock levels?).

Types of Relationships Between Business Variables

1. **Positive Relationship**: When one variable increases, the other also increases. For example, higher customer satisfaction ratings lead to more repeat purchases.

2. **Negative Relationship**: When one variable increases, the other decreases. For example, an increase in product price may lead to a decrease in the number of units sold.

3. **No Relationship**: When changes in one variable do not predict changes in another variable. For example, the number of customers visiting a store may not correlate with the store's marketing budget.

4. **Non-linear Relationship**: Sometimes, the relationship between two variables might not be linear, meaning the change in one variable is not proportional to the change in the other variable.

Methods for Assessing Relationships

1. **Correlation**: Measures the strength and direction of the linear relationship between two variables. Common correlation methods include:

   o **Pearson Correlation**: Assumes a linear relationship and is sensitive to outliers.

o **Spearman Rank Correlation**: Used for ordinal data or non-linear relationships.

2. **Regression Analysis**: Used to model and understand the relationship between a dependent variable and one or more independent variables. This is typically used for prediction purposes.

3. **Data Visualization**: Plotting data using scatter plots, bar charts, or line graphs to visually inspect relationships between variables.

4. **Chi-Square Test**: Used for assessing relationships between categorical variables.

Example: Assessing the Relationship Between Advertising Spend and Sales Performance

Business Scenario:

A company wants to assess the relationship between its **monthly advertising spend** and **sales revenue** over the past 6 months. The company aims to understand if higher advertising spend leads to increased sales.

Sample Data: Advertising Spend vs. Sales Revenue

Month	Advertising Spend ($)	Sales Revenue ($)
January	10,000	50,000
February	12,000	55,000
March	15,000	60,000
April	18,000	70,000
May	20,000	80,000
June	22,000	90,000

- **Advertising Spend** is an independent variable, representing the company's investment in marketing.

- **Sales Revenue** is the dependent variable, representing the income generated from sales.

Analyzing the Relationship: Steps

1. **Visual Inspection**: A **scatter plot** would help visualize the relationship between advertising spend and sales revenue. If the points form a line that ascends from left to right, it suggests a positive correlation.

2. **Correlation Analysis**: Calculate the **Pearson correlation** to measure the strength and direction of the linear relationship between advertising spend and sales revenue.

3. **Regression Analysis**: A **simple linear regression** could be used to predict sales revenue based on advertising spend.

Hypothetical Results

Step 1: Scatter Plot Interpretation (Visualizing Data)

The scatter plot shows a clear upward trend, where **higher advertising spend** corresponds to **higher sales revenue**. This visually suggests a positive relationship.

Step 2: Correlation Analysis

Metric	Value
Pearson Correlation Coefficient	**0.99**
P-value	**0.0002**

- **Pearson Correlation (0.99)**: This indicates a **very strong positive linear relationship** between **advertising spend** and **sales revenue**. As advertising spend increases, sales revenue increases proportionally.

- **P-value (0.0002)**: The p-value is very small (less than 0.05), indicating that the correlation is statistically significant and not due to random chance.

Step 3: Regression Analysis

Using regression analysis, we estimate the relationship between advertising spend and sales revenue:

Metric	Value
Intercept (constant)	30,000
Slope (coefficient)	2.5
R-squared	0.98

- **Intercept (30,000)**: This is the baseline sales revenue when advertising spend is zero. It suggests that even without advertising spend, the company would still have $30,000 in sales revenue.

- **Slope (2.5)**: This indicates that for every **$1 increase in advertising spend**, sales revenue increases by **$2.50**. This shows a strong positive relationship between the two variables.

- **R-squared (0.98)**: This suggests that **98% of the variation** in sales revenue can be explained by advertising spend. This is a very high proportion, indicating that advertising spend is a strong predictor of sales revenue.

Explanation of Results:

- **Strong Positive Correlation**: The **Pearson correlation coefficient of 0.99** confirms that there is a very strong positive linear relationship between **advertising spend** and **sales revenue**. This means that as the company increases its advertising budget, sales revenue tends to increase as well, in a linear manner.

- **Significance of the Relationship**: The **p-value of 0.0002** indicates that the relationship between advertising spend and sales revenue is statistically significant. This means that the observed correlation is unlikely to have happened by chance.

- **Regression Results**:

  o The **intercept of $30,000** tells us that even without any advertising spend, the company would still generate $30,000 in sales.

  o The **slope of 2.5** indicates that every additional dollar spent on advertising increases sales revenue by $2.50. This highlights the return on investment (ROI) for the company's advertising spend.

  o The **R-squared value of 0.98** shows that advertising spend explains 98% of the variation in sales revenue. This is a strong indication that advertising spend is a major driver of sales, and the company could make decisions about increasing its budget to drive further sales growth.

Business Insights and Decisions:

- **Increased Advertising Spend**: Since there is a strong positive relationship, the company could consider increasing its advertising budget to boost sales further. The regression model suggests that a $1 increase in advertising spend leads to a $2.50 increase in sales revenue.

- **Budget Allocation**: Given the strong **R-squared value**, the company can be confident that its marketing efforts are highly effective in driving sales. The company might allocate more of its budget to advertising to maximize revenue.

- **Predictive Insights**: The company can use the regression equation to forecast sales revenue based on different advertising budgets. For example, if the company plans to increase its advertising spend to $25,000, the model suggests the expected sales revenue could be:

$$\textbf{Sales Revenue=30,000+2.5×25,000=107,500}$$

Caution: Although the correlation and regression results are strong, the company should also consider other external factors (like market trends, seasonality, competition, etc.) that could influence sales, to avoid overreliance on advertising spend alone.

Conclusion:

In this example, the company found a **strong positive correlation** between **advertising spend** and **sales revenue**. The results of the correlation and regression analysis provide valuable insights into how advertising impacts sales and offer predictive power for decision-making. However, businesses should always consider additional factors and validate assumptions before making major decisions based solely on statistical analysis.

7.3 Implications of Correlation in Strategy Formulation

In Business Analytics, **correlation** is a powerful tool for understanding the relationship between two or more variables. It helps businesses identify **patterns, trends**, and **dependencies** that can drive strategic decisions. By examining the strength and direction of correlations, businesses can **optimize operations, allocate resources more effectively**, and **predict future outcomes**.

Key Implications of Correlation in Business Strategy:

1. **Resource Allocation**: Understanding correlations can guide how a business allocates resources, such as marketing budget, manpower, or production capacity. For example, if higher marketing spend correlates with increased sales, the business might decide to increase its marketing budget to boost revenue.

2. **Performance Monitoring**: Correlation analysis can help businesses track key performance indicators (KPIs) and identify areas that need attention. For example, if employee satisfaction strongly correlates with customer satisfaction, a company might invest in employee well-being programs to improve overall service quality.

3. **Optimization of Processes**: By analyzing the relationships between different operational factors, businesses can improve efficiency. For example, if there's a strong correlation between inventory turnover and sales, businesses can optimize stock levels to match demand more accurately.

4. **Predictive Modeling and Forecasting**: Correlation analysis provides insights that can be used for building predictive models. For instance, if historical data shows a strong correlation between sales performance and the time of year (e.g., holiday season), businesses can forecast sales for future periods based on seasonal trends.

5. **Risk Assessment and Management**: Correlation can also help identify risks. For example, if a certain variable, like supplier delays, negatively correlates with on-time product delivery, businesses can take preemptive steps to mitigate the risk of delays.

6. **Market Segmentation**: Correlation analysis can help identify customer segments that behave similarly. For instance, if **age** correlates strongly with **purchasing behavior**, businesses can tailor marketing strategies for different age groups.

Types of Correlation That Can Influence Business Strategy:

- **Positive Correlation**: A positive correlation means that as one variable increases, the other variable also increases. This can be beneficial for businesses aiming to **scale operations** or **increase revenues** by strategically aligning related factors.

- **Negative Correlation**: A negative correlation means that as one variable increases, the other decreases. Businesses can use this information to **avoid or minimize losses**, like reducing costs associated with variables that negatively affect profits.

- **No Correlation**: Sometimes there is no significant correlation between variables, which suggests that **certain factors do not influence each other**. This insight can help businesses **focus on more impactful relationships**.

Example: Assessing the Correlation Between Marketing Spend and Sales Revenue

Business Scenario:

A retail company wants to assess whether there is a relationship between its **monthly marketing spend** and **sales revenue**. The company hopes to identify if increasing marketing spending will lead to a corresponding increase in sales. If a strong positive correlation exists, the company might increase its marketing budget for future growth.

Sample Data: Marketing Spend and Sales Revenue

Month	Marketing Spend ($)	Sales Revenue ($)
January	15,000	50,000
February	18,000	55,000
March	20,000	60,000
April	25,000	70,000
May	30,000	80,000
June	35,000	85,000

- **Marketing Spend**: This is the amount the company invests in its marketing activities.

- **Sales Revenue**: This represents the total sales made by the company each month.

Analysis: Interpreting the Correlation Between Marketing Spend and Sales Revenue

Step 1: Visual Inspection

By plotting the data on a **scatter plot**, we can visually inspect whether there is an upward trend between marketing spend and sales revenue. If the points appear to form a straight line that ascends from left to right, it suggests a positive correlation.

Step 2: Correlation Analysis

Metric	Value
Pearson Correlation Coefficient	0.98
P-value	0.0003

- **Pearson Correlation Coefficient (0.98)**: This value indicates a **very strong positive linear relationship** between **marketing spend** and **sales revenue**. As marketing spend increases, sales revenue also increases. The strong correlation suggests that increasing the marketing budget is likely to lead to higher sales.

- **P-value (0.0003)**: The p-value is significantly less than the standard threshold of 0.05, indicating that the relationship between marketing spend and sales revenue is statistically significant. This means the observed correlation is unlikely to have occurred by chance.

Step 3: Regression Analysis (for Further Insights)

To better understand the relationship, we could also perform **regression analysis** to predict sales revenue based on marketing spend.

Metric	Value
Intercept (constant)	40,000
Slope (coefficient)	1.5
R-squared	0.96

- **Intercept (40,000)**: This is the base sales revenue when marketing spend is zero. It suggests that the company would still generate $40,000 in sales without any marketing spend, indicating a baseline level of sales.

- **Slope (1.5)**: This means that for every additional **$1 spent on marketing**, the company sees a **$1.50 increase in sales revenue**. This gives the company an insight into the return on investment (ROI) for marketing spend.

- **R-squared (0.96)**: This indicates that **96% of the variation** in sales revenue can be explained by the marketing spend. This suggests that marketing spend is a key driver of sales performance, and that increasing the marketing budget is likely to have a strong impact on sales revenue.

Explanation of Results:

1. **Strong Positive Relationship**: The **Pearson correlation of 0.98** suggests a very strong linear relationship between marketing spend and sales revenue. This means that as marketing spend increases, sales revenue also increases significantly. This insight can inform the company's decision to increase its marketing budget, expecting a proportionate increase in sales.

2. **Statistical Significance**: The **p-value of 0.0003** confirms that this correlation is statistically significant. The company can be confident that the observed relationship between marketing spend and sales revenue is not due to random chance.

3. **Return on Investment (ROI)**: The **slope of 1.5** in the regression analysis suggests that for every dollar invested in marketing, the company earns an additional $1.50 in sales. This indicates a **strong return on investment** and provides a basis for the company to justify increasing the marketing budget.

4. **Predictive Power**: The **R-squared value of 0.96** means that marketing spend accounts for 96% of the variation in sales revenue. This high R-squared value suggests that marketing is a major factor driving sales, and increasing the marketing budget is likely to result in higher sales revenue.

Business Insights and Strategy Formulation:

- **Increase Marketing Budget**: Based on the strong correlation and regression analysis, the company could consider increasing its marketing spend to drive further sales growth. Since marketing spend has a strong positive effect on sales, investing more in advertising and promotions can help the company achieve higher revenues.

- **Forecasting and Budget Planning**: With the regression model, the company can predict future sales revenue based on different marketing budgets. For example, if the company plans to increase its marketing budget to $40,000 in the next quarter, it can expect sales revenue to increase by $60,000 (since $40,000 x 1.5 = $60,000).

- **Optimize Marketing Strategy**: The company can also use the insights from the analysis to **optimize its marketing strategy**. For example, if some marketing channels (such as online ads or social media) yield a better ROI than others, the company can reallocate its marketing budget towards those channels for maximum effectiveness.

- **Monitoring ROI**: With a strong understanding of the **ROI of marketing spend**, the company can continuously monitor its marketing campaigns and adjust the budget to ensure optimal performance. The company might also track changes in **sales revenue** over time to see if the ROI remains consistent, or if diminishing returns occur at higher levels of spend.

Conclusion:

In this example, the **strong positive correlation** between **marketing spend** and **sales revenue** gives the company a clear strategy for growth. By understanding the relationship between these variables, the company can **optimize its marketing budget**, **predict sales growth**, and ensure a high return on investment. Moreover, the company can continuously refine its strategy to maximize sales and optimize resource allocation based on the insights derived from the correlation analysis.

7.4 Correlation test on sample business data

Apply the Correlation test on sample business data (Refer Chapter 1.7) to compare the **Sales Amount**, **Target Sales**, and **Marketing Spend**. Here are the results and the business decisions:

Correlation Matrix

	Sales Amount	Target Sales	Marketing Spend
Sales Amount	1.000	0.955	0.783
Target Sales	0.955	1.000	0.795
Marketing Spend	0.783	0.795	1.000

Discussion of Results

1. **Sales Amount and Target Sales**:

    - **Correlation Coefficient**: 0.955

    - **Interpretation**: There is a very strong positive correlation between sales amount and target sales. This indicates that as target sales increase, the actual sales amount tends to increase as well.

2. **Sales Amount and Marketing Spend**:

    - **Correlation Coefficient**: 0.783

    - **Interpretation**: There is a strong positive correlation between sales amount and marketing spend. This suggests that higher marketing spend is associated with higher sales amounts.

3. **Target Sales and Marketing Spend**:

    - **Correlation Coefficient**: 0.795

    - **Interpretation**: There is a strong positive correlation between target sales and marketing spend. This indicates that higher marketing spend is associated with higher target sales.

Business Implications and Decisions

1. **Performance Alignment**:

    - The strong correlation between sales amount and target sales suggests that the targets set are realistic and aligned with actual sales performance. This can help in setting future targets and evaluating performance.

2. **Marketing Effectiveness**:

   - The strong correlation between marketing spend and both sales amount and target sales indicates that marketing efforts are effective in driving sales. The business should continue to invest in marketing to maintain and potentially increase sales.

3. **Resource Allocation**:

   - Understanding the impact of marketing spend on sales can help in better resource allocation. The business can optimize its marketing budget to achieve the best return on investment.

4. **Strategic Planning**:

   - The insights from the correlation analysis can inform strategic decisions such as setting sales targets, planning marketing campaigns, and optimizing resource allocation to achieve growth targets.

5. **Performance Monitoring**:

   - Regular monitoring of these correlations can help the business identify trends and make data-driven decisions. This ongoing analysis can ensure that strategies remain effective and are adjusted as needed.

By leveraging these statistical insights, businesses can make informed decisions to optimize sales performance and achieve growth targets.

8. Linear Regression in Business Analytics: *To predict an outcome (dependent variable) based on the value(s) of one or more predictors (independent variables)*

Linear Regression is a powerful statistical tool used in Business Analytics to model the relationship between a dependent variable and one or more independent variables. In simple terms, it helps businesses predict an outcome (dependent variable) based on the value(s) of one or more predictors (independent variables). Linear regression is most commonly used when the relationship between the variables is assumed to be **linear** (i.e., a straight-line relationship).

Key Concepts:

- **Dependent Variable (Target)**: The outcome we want to predict or explain (e.g., sales revenue, customer churn).

- **Independent Variable (Predictor)**: The factor(s) used to predict the dependent variable (e.g., advertising spend, customer age).

- **Linear Relationship**: A relationship between the variables that can be approximated by a straight line (i.e., the dependent variable changes at a constant rate with respect to the independent variable).

- **Intercept and Slope**: In linear regression, the relationship is modeled by an equation of the form:

$$Y = \beta_0 + \beta_1 X$$

Where:

- o   Y is the dependent variable (what we are predicting),

- o   X is the independent variable (predictor),

- o β_0 is the intercept (the value of Y when X=0),

- o β_1 is the slope (the rate of change in Y for a unit change in X).

Applications of Linear Regression in Business:

- **Sales Forecasting**: Predicting future sales based on factors like advertising spend, product prices, and promotional efforts.

- **Customer Lifetime Value (CLV)**: Estimating the future value of a customer based on past purchasing behavior.

- **Budgeting**: Estimating the required budget to achieve a desired level of output or performance.

- **Risk Assessment**: Predicting potential risks or losses based on certain business factors.

Example: Predicting Sales Based on Advertising Spend

Business Scenario:

A retail company wants to predict its **monthly sales revenue** based on the **monthly advertising spend**. The company has historical data for the past 6 months and wants to understand how much advertising spend is likely to affect sales revenue.

Sample Data: Advertising Spend vs. Sales Revenue

Month	Advertising Spend ($)	Sales Revenue ($)
January	10,000	50,000
February	12,000	55,000
March	15,000	60,000
April	18,000	70,000
May	20,000	75,000
June	22,000	80,000

- **Advertising Spend** is the independent variable, representing the company's investment in marketing efforts.

- **Sales Revenue** is the dependent variable, representing the total income generated from sales.

Objective:

The objective is to create a linear regression model that predicts **Sales Revenue** based on the **Advertising Spend**.

Step 1: Visual Inspection

We begin by plotting the data on a **scatter plot** with **Advertising Spend** on the x-axis and **Sales Revenue** on the y-axis. If the points appear to align in an upward direction, it suggests that there is a positive linear relationship between advertising spend and sales revenue.

Step 2: Linear Regression Model Interpretation

Results of the Linear Regression Model

Metric	Value

Intercept (β_0)	40,000
Slope (β_1)	2
R-squared	0.98
P-value	0.0004

- **Intercept (β_0 = 40,000)**: The intercept represents the expected sales revenue when **Advertising Spend is zero**. In this case, even if the company spends nothing on advertising, it is estimated to generate **$40,000** in sales. This could be due to factors such as brand loyalty or organic traffic.

- **Slope (β_1 = 2.0)**: The slope represents the rate of change in sales revenue for each additional dollar spent on advertising. In this case, for each **$1 increase in advertising spend**, sales revenue increases by **$2**. This suggests that advertising spend has a significant positive effect on sales, and for every dollar invested in advertising, the company can expect a $2 return in sales revenue.

- **R-squared (0.98)**: The **R-squared** value of 0.98 means that **98% of the variability in sales revenue** can be explained by the amount spent on advertising. This is a very high value, indicating that advertising spend is a strong predictor of sales revenue and that the linear regression model fits the data very well.

- **P-value (0.0004)**: The **p-value** is very small (less than the typical threshold of 0.05), indicating that the relationship between advertising spend and sales revenue is statistically significant. In other words, the observed correlation is unlikely to have occurred by chance.

Step 3: Predictions

The company can now use the **linear regression equation** to predict sales revenue based on different levels of advertising spend. The equation is:

$$\text{Sales Revenue} = 40,000 + 2 \times (\text{Advertising Spend})$$

Example Prediction:

If the company plans to increase its **advertising spend to $25,000** next month, we can use the regression model to predict the sales revenue:

$$\text{Sales Revenue} = 40,000 + 2 \times 25,000 = 90,000$$

This means that, based on the model, the company can expect **$90,000** in sales revenue if it spends **$25,000** on advertising.

Explanation of Results:

1. **Intercept (40,000)**: This represents the **base level of sales revenue** that the company can expect without any advertising spend. It suggests that even without any additional marketing efforts, the company would still generate $40,000 in sales due to factors like brand reputation, returning customers, and organic market presence.

2. **Slope (2.0)**: This indicates a strong **positive relationship** between advertising spend and sales revenue. Specifically, for every additional **$1 spent on advertising**, sales revenue increases by **$2**. The business can use this insight to justify increased marketing investments, knowing that they will likely yield higher returns.

3. **R-squared (0.98)**: The model explains **98%** of the variability in sales revenue based on advertising spend. This means that advertising spend is a very important driver of sales, and the linear regression model provides an **accurate fit** to the data.

4. **P-value (0.0004)**: The small p-value confirms that the relationship between advertising spend and sales revenue is **statistically significant**. This means that the observed relationship is not due to random chance, and the company can rely on this model for decision-making.

Business Insights and Strategy Formulation:

- **Optimizing Marketing Spend**: The company can use the **linear regression model** to forecast sales revenue for different advertising budgets. For example, if the company expects to invest more in marketing, it can use the model to project the sales revenue it can expect as a result.

- **Resource Allocation**: Since advertising spend has a **strong impact on sales**, the company might decide to allocate a higher portion of its budget to marketing in the future. The **slope of 2.0** implies that increasing the marketing budget will yield significant returns in terms of sales revenue.

- **Sales Forecasting**: The company can use the regression equation to **predict sales** for upcoming months based on their planned advertising budget. For instance, if they want to predict sales revenue for next quarter, they can input the estimated advertising spend for each month into the equation.

- **ROI Analysis**: The company can also evaluate the **return on investment (ROI)** for advertising spend by comparing the sales revenue generated to the amount spent on advertising. Since the regression model shows a $2 return for every $1 spent, this is a favorable ROI, justifying continued or increased investment in advertising.

Conclusion:

In this example, the company used **linear regression** to model the relationship between **advertising spend** and **sales revenue**. The **strong positive correlation** between these two variables (with a high **R-squared** of 0.98) suggests that **advertising is a key driver of sales**. The company can use the regression model to **forecast future sales, optimize marketing spend**, and make data-driven decisions to maximize revenue. The statistical significance of the results provides confidence in the predictive power of the model, helping the company strategize effectively for future growth.

8.1 Exploring Linear Regression Analysis in Business Context

Linear regression analysis is a statistical method used to model and analyze the relationship between one dependent variable (also known as the response or target variable) and one or more independent variables (also known as predictors or features). It is a fundamental technique in business analytics for predicting outcomes and understanding the relationships between different business factors.

Linear regression assumes a **linear relationship** between the independent variables and the dependent variable, meaning that changes in the independent variables are expected to cause proportional changes in the dependent variable. The purpose of linear regression is to develop a model that allows businesses to predict future values or outcomes based on known data.

Key Components of Linear Regression:

1. **Dependent Variable (Target)**: This is the outcome variable that you are trying to predict. For example, sales revenue, customer satisfaction, or profit.

2. **Independent Variable (Predictor)**: These are the input variables used to predict the dependent variable. For example, marketing spend, product price, or advertising efforts.

3. **Linear Relationship**: The relationship between the dependent and independent variables is assumed to be linear, meaning that the dependent variable changes in a constant manner as the independent variable changes.

4. **Regression Equation**: In simple linear regression, the relationship is expressed as a straight line. The general form of the equation is:

$$Y = \beta_0 + \beta_1 X$$

Where:

o Y is the dependent variable (what you are predicting),

o β_0 is the intercept (value of Y when X=0),

o β_1 is the slope (rate of change in Y as X changes),

o X is the independent variable (the predictor).

5. **Error Term (Residuals)**: The difference between the observed value and the predicted value. A smaller error means the model is a better fit for the data.

Importance of Linear Regression in Business Analytics:

- **Predictive Analytics**: Businesses can use linear regression to predict future outcomes, such as sales, demand, customer behavior, and product pricing, based on historical data.

- **Decision Making**: It helps decision-makers understand how changes in independent variables (like marketing budget or price changes) will impact business outcomes (such as revenue or customer acquisition).

- **Trend Identification**: Linear regression identifies trends and patterns in data, making it easier for businesses to forecast future performance and adjust strategies accordingly.

- **Resource Allocation**: By understanding the impact of various factors on business performance, businesses can allocate resources more efficiently to maximize returns.

Types of Linear Regression:

- **Simple Linear Regression**: Involves one independent variable and one dependent variable. The relationship is modeled as a straight line.

- **Multiple Linear Regression**: Involves more than one independent variable, providing a more complex model that can capture the relationship between several factors and the dependent variable.

Example: Predicting Sales Based on Advertising Spend (Simple Linear Regression)

Business Scenario:

A retail company wants to understand how their **advertising spend** impacts their **sales revenue**. They collect data on their monthly advertising spend and sales revenue over the last 6 months and want to use this data to predict future sales based on planned advertising expenditure.

Sample Data: Advertising Spend vs. Sales Revenue

Month	Advertising Spend ($)	Sales Revenue ($)
January	10,000	50,000
February	12,000	55,000
March	15,000	60,000

April	18,000	70,000
May	20,000	75,000
June	22,000	80,000

- **Advertising Spend** is the independent variable (predictor), which represents the amount the company spends on advertising each month.

- **Sales Revenue** is the dependent variable (response), representing the total sales generated from the advertising efforts.

Objective:

The objective is to create a linear regression model to predict **sales revenue** based on **advertising spend**.

Results of Linear Regression Analysis:

Metric	Value
Intercept (β_0)	40,000
Slope (β_1)	2
R-squared	0.98
P-value	0.0002

Interpretation of Results:

1. **Intercept (β_0 = 40,000):** The intercept of 40,000 suggests that, if the company were to spend **zero** on advertising, they would still expect to generate **$40,000** in sales revenue. This might be due to existing customer base, repeat purchases, or brand loyalty. The intercept represents the baseline sales revenue.

2. **Slope (β_1 = 2.0):** The slope of 2.0 means that for every **$1 increase in advertising spend**, the company can expect **$2 increase in sales revenue**. This indicates that advertising has a strong positive impact on sales. The company can interpret this as a very efficient return on investment (ROI) in advertising, where each dollar spent generates $2 in additional revenue.

3. **R-squared (0.98):** The **R-squared value** of 0.98 indicates that **98%** of the variation in sales revenue can be explained by the amount spent on advertising. This is a very strong fit, suggesting that advertising spend is a major factor driving sales performance in this case. The remaining 2% of the variation could be attributed to other factors not included in the model.

4. **P-value (0.0002):** The **p-value** of 0.0002 is significantly smaller than the standard threshold of 0.05, indicating that the relationship between advertising spend and sales revenue is **statistically significant**. This means that the observed relationship between these two variables is highly

unlikely to have occurred by random chance, and the model can be relied upon to make predictions.

Predicting Future Sales:

Using the regression equation:

$$\text{Sales Revenue} = 40,000 + 2 \times (\text{Advertising Spend})$$

We can predict the sales revenue for a future advertising spend of $25,000:

$$\text{Sales Revenue} = 40,000 + 2 \times 25,000 = 90,000$$

Therefore, if the company spends **$25,000** on advertising in the future, the model predicts that sales revenue will be **$90,000**.

Business Insights and Strategy Formulation:

1. **Forecasting Sales**: The regression model allows the company to predict future sales based on different levels of advertising spend. By adjusting the marketing budget, the company can forecast how much additional revenue they could generate.

2. **Optimizing Advertising Spend**: The company now knows that for every **$1** spent on advertising, they can expect to generate **$2** in sales. This high return on investment suggests that increasing the advertising budget would be a good strategy for increasing sales, provided the company has the resources to allocate to marketing.

3. **Resource Allocation**: With an **R-squared of 0.98**, the company can confidently invest more in advertising, knowing that the relationship between advertising and sales is very strong. If the company aims to achieve specific sales targets, they can calculate the necessary advertising spend using the regression equation.

4. **Understanding Sales Drivers**: The analysis shows that **advertising spend** is a key driver of sales revenue, but the company may also want to explore other factors (like customer demographics, seasonal trends, or product pricing) that could influence sales. A **multiple linear regression** model, which includes more predictors, could provide a more comprehensive view.

Conclusion:

In this example, linear regression was used to model the relationship between **advertising spend** and **sales revenue**. The analysis revealed that advertising has a strong positive effect on sales, with a very high **R-squared value** indicating a strong fit of the model. By using the regression equation, the company can confidently predict sales revenue for different levels of advertising spend and make data-driven decisions about future marketing investments. The results also provide insight into the **ROI of advertising spend**, helping the company optimize its marketing strategy to maximize revenue.

8.2 Building and Evaluating Regression Models

Building and evaluating regression models is a core aspect of **Business Analytics**. Regression models are used to understand the relationship between a **dependent variable** (the outcome we want to predict or explain) and one or more **independent variables** (the predictors or features that help in predicting the outcome). The goal is to develop a model that can accurately predict future outcomes and inform business decisions based on historical data.

Key Steps in Building and Evaluating Regression Models:

1. **Data Collection and Preparation**:
    - Collect historical data that includes both dependent and independent variables.
    - Clean the data by handling missing values, removing outliers, and transforming variables as necessary.

2. **Exploratory Data Analysis (EDA)**:
    - Visualize the relationships between variables to understand the trends and patterns.
    - Assess the correlation between the independent variables and the dependent variable.

3. **Model Building**:
    - Choose the appropriate regression type (e.g., **simple linear regression**, **multiple linear regression**, etc.) based on the problem at hand.
    - Fit the regression model to the data by estimating the parameters (intercept and coefficients).

4. **Model Evaluation**:
    - Evaluate the model's performance using key metrics such as **R-squared, p-values, adjusted R-squared**, and **Mean Squared Error (MSE)**.
    - Check assumptions such as linearity, independence, homoscedasticity (constant variance), and normality of errors.

5. **Model Refinement**:
    - If necessary, refine the model by adjusting the predictor variables, using transformations, or using regularization techniques like **Lasso** or **Ridge Regression**.

6. **Prediction and Insights**:

  o   Once the model is built and evaluated, use it to make predictions and provide actionable insights for business decision-making.

Example: Predicting Sales Based on Advertising Spend and Store Size

Business Scenario:

A retail company wants to understand the impact of **advertising spend** and **store size** on its **monthly sales revenue**. The company wants to build a regression model that will help predict sales revenue for future months based on how much is spent on advertising and the size of the stores.

Sample Data: Advertising Spend, Store Size, and Sales Revenue

Month	Advertising Spend ($)	Store Size (sq ft)	Sales Revenue ($)
January	10,000	1,500	50,000
February	12,000	1,600	55,000
March	15,000	1,800	60,000
April	18,000	2,000	70,000
May	20,000	2,200	75,000
June	22,000	2,400	80,000

- **Advertising Spend** and **Store Size** are the **independent variables**.
- **Sales Revenue** is the **dependent variable** that the company wants to predict.

Step 1: Exploratory Data Analysis (EDA)

Before building the model, we would look at the data to see if there are any obvious patterns:

- **Visualize the data** using scatter plots to check if there is a clear relationship between each independent variable (advertising spend and store size) and sales revenue.
- **Correlation Analysis**: Calculate the correlation coefficients to see how strongly each independent variable is related to sales revenue.

Step 2: Building the Regression Model

Using the data, we build a **multiple linear regression model** with **Advertising Spend** and **Store Size** as the independent variables. The goal is to predict **Sales Revenue**.

The regression equation is typically:

$$\text{Sales Revenue} = \beta_0 + \beta_1 \times \text{Advertising Spend} + \beta_2 \times \text{Store Size}$$

Where:

- β_0 is the intercept (base sales revenue when advertising spend and store size are zero).

- β_1 is the coefficient for advertising spend (how much sales revenue increases for every additional dollar spent on advertising).

- β_2 is the coefficient for store size (how much sales revenue increases for every additional square foot of store size).

Step 3: Evaluating the Model

After fitting the model to the data, we evaluate the model's performance by looking at the following metrics:

1. **R-squared (Coefficient of Determination)**: This tells us how well the independent variables explain the variation in the dependent variable (sales revenue). An **R-squared** value close to 1 indicates a good fit.

2. **P-value**: This assesses the significance of each predictor (independent variable). A p-value less than 0.05 indicates that the variable is statistically significant.

3. **Adjusted R-squared**: This adjusts the R-squared for the number of predictors in the model. It is a better measure when there are multiple predictors.

4. **F-statistic**: This tests whether at least one of the predictors is significantly related to the dependent variable.

5. **Standard Error**: This measures the accuracy of the model's predictions. Smaller values indicate better predictive accuracy.

Step 4: Model Results

Example Results:

Metric	Value
Intercept (β_0)	30,000
Advertising Spend (β_1)	2.5
Store Size (β_2)	15
R-squared	0.97
Adjusted R-squared	0.96
P-value (Advertising Spend)	0.002
P-value (Store Size)	0.004

F-statistic	45.6
Standard Error	2,000

Interpretation of Results:

1. **Intercept ($\beta_0 = 30,000$):**

   o The intercept suggests that, even if the company spends no money on advertising and the store has no size (i.e., hypothetically, no store), it can expect a base level of **$30,000** in sales revenue. This could be attributed to factors like repeat customers or brand recognition.

2. **Advertising Spend ($\beta_1 = 2.5$):**

   o The coefficient for **Advertising Spend** tells us that for each additional dollar spent on advertising, the company can expect an increase of **$2.5** in sales revenue. This shows that advertising has a positive and significant impact on sales revenue.

3. **Store Size ($\beta_2 = 15$):**

   o The coefficient for **Store Size** suggests that for each additional square foot of store size, the company can expect **$15** more in sales revenue. This indicates that larger stores tend to generate higher sales, which is typical for businesses where product variety and customer experience improve with store size.

4. **R-squared (0.97):**

   o An **R-squared value of 0.97** indicates that **97%** of the variation in sales revenue can be explained by advertising spend and store size. This is a very strong model fit, meaning that the model is very effective at predicting sales revenue based on the given predictors.

5. **Adjusted R-squared (0.96):**

   o The **adjusted R-squared** value of 0.96 accounts for the number of predictors in the model and is also quite high. This means that even though we have two predictors, the model still provides a very reliable explanation of the variation in sales revenue.

6. **P-values:**

   o The **p-values** for both advertising spend (**0.002**) and store size (**0.004**) are both much less than the typical significance level of 0.05. This indicates that both **advertising spend** and **store size** are

statistically significant predictors of sales revenue. These variables have a strong, proven relationship with sales.

7. **F-statistic (45.6)**:

   o The **F-statistic** value is quite high, which suggests that the overall regression model is significant, and at least one of the independent variables is having a meaningful impact on sales revenue.

8. **Standard Error (2,000)**:

   o The **standard error** of **$2,000** indicates the typical deviation between the actual sales revenue and the predicted sales revenue. A smaller standard error suggests that the model's predictions are relatively accurate.

Step 5: Business Insights and Strategy Formulation

1. **Marketing Strategy**: Based on the coefficient for **Advertising Spend**, the company can decide how much to invest in advertising to achieve desired sales revenue. Since each dollar spent on advertising increases sales by $2.5, the company can estimate the returns on marketing investments.

2. **Store Expansion**: Given that **store size** significantly influences sales revenue, the company may consider expanding store size or investing in larger retail spaces to boost sales.

3. **Predictive Analytics**: The company can use the regression model to predict sales revenue for different levels of **advertising spend** and **store size** in future months. This helps with forecasting and strategic planning.

4. **Resource Allocation**: The company can allocate resources more efficiently by focusing on the variables that have the most impact on sales. For instance, if expanding store size has a significant impact, they may prioritize finding larger retail spaces in key locations.

Conclusion:

Building and evaluating regression models enables businesses to make data-driven decisions based on historical data. In this example, a **multiple linear regression** model was built to predict sales revenue based on **advertising spend** and **store size**. The results showed that both factors are statistically significant and have a strong relationship with sales. With this model, the company can make more informed decisions about marketing investments and store expansion to optimize revenue.

8.3 Applications in Sales Forecasting and Market Analysis

Sales Forecasting and **Market Analysis** are critical functions in Business Analytics. These processes help organizations predict future sales, evaluate market trends, and make informed decisions that can optimize performance. By analyzing historical data and recognizing patterns, businesses can gain insights into customer behavior, product demand, and market conditions.

Key Applications:

1. **Sales Forecasting:**

   o Sales forecasting helps businesses predict future sales over a specific time period. Accurate forecasts enable companies to manage inventory, staffing, budgeting, and overall strategy.

   o It involves using historical sales data to identify trends, patterns, and seasonality, which can then be extrapolated to forecast future sales.

   o Various techniques such as moving averages, exponential smoothing, and regression analysis can be used for forecasting.

2. **Market Analysis:**

   o Market analysis involves assessing and interpreting data related to market conditions, customer preferences, competitor activities, and industry trends.

   o It helps businesses identify growth opportunities, understand competitive dynamics, and evaluate the effectiveness of marketing strategies.

   o Market analysis can involve segmentation of customers, analyzing product sales by region, and measuring the impact of different marketing channels.

Example: Sales Forecasting for a Retail Company

Business Scenario:

A retail company wants to forecast its sales for the next quarter. The company has collected data on its monthly sales over the last year. Based on this data, the company aims to predict future sales and make decisions about inventory and staffing.

Sample Data: Monthly Sales Data for the Last Year

Month	Sales ($)
January	45,000
February	47,000
March	49,000
April	52,000
May	54,000
June	55,000
July	58,000
August	60,000
September	62,000
October	64,000
November	66,000
December	68,000

In this example, the company has monthly sales data for the past year. The goal is to use this data to forecast the sales for the next quarter (January, February, March).

Step 1: Exploratory Data Analysis (EDA)

- **Trend and Seasonality**: The company first needs to identify whether there is any trend or seasonality in the sales data. For example, does the company see a pattern of increasing sales month by month, or are there certain months that consistently show higher or lower sales?

- **Visualization**: A time-series plot of the sales data will help to visually assess trends and seasonality. By looking at the chart, the company can determine if there is a consistent upward trend in sales or if sales fluctuate in a cyclical pattern.

Step 2: Forecasting Model

- **Simple Moving Average**: One simple approach to forecasting is the moving average method, where future sales are predicted by averaging the sales from the previous few months. This method helps smooth out short-term fluctuations and highlight longer-term trends.

- **Linear Regression**: For more sophisticated forecasting, the company may use **linear regression** to model the relationship between the time variable (e.g., months) and sales. This can help predict future sales based on past trends.

Step 3: Model Evaluation

- **Accuracy**: The accuracy of the model is evaluated by comparing the predicted sales with actual sales data over a period. If the forecasted sales are close to the actual sales, the model is considered accurate.

- **Forecast Error**: Companies often evaluate the forecast error, which is the difference between the actual sales and predicted sales. Smaller errors indicate a better forecast.

Step 4: Forecasting Results

Results of Sales Forecasting for the Next Quarter:

Month	Actual Sales ($)	Predicted Sales ($)
January	45,000	50,000
February	47,000	52,000
March	49,000	55,000

Explanation of Results:

1. **Trend**: The sales data from the previous year indicates a general **upward trend** in sales, with an increase of about **$2,000 to $3,000** per month. This trend suggests that sales are likely to continue growing, assuming no major changes in the market or external factors.

2. **Forecast**: The model uses this upward trend to predict future sales. For example:

   o **January** sales are predicted to be $50,000, which is slightly higher than the actual sales of $45,000 in the same month of the previous year.

   o **February** sales are forecasted at $52,000, which is also higher than the actual sales in February of the previous year ($47,000).

   o **March** sales are predicted to be $55,000, continuing the trend of gradual growth.

3. **Forecast Accuracy**: The forecast for **January** ($50,000) is fairly close to the actual sales ($45,000), but it's an overestimate. Similarly, the forecast for **February** and **March** is slightly higher than actual sales from the previous year. This is typical for forecasting models that use trends from historical data and may not always account for other factors like promotions or external market conditions.

4. **Business Implications**:

   o The company can use these predictions to **plan inventory levels**, ensuring they have sufficient stock to meet the anticipated sales.

- o Staffing needs can also be adjusted based on the predicted increase in sales.

- o Marketing strategies can be aligned with the forecasted sales periods, potentially offering promotions or discounts in months where sales are expected to dip or remain flat.

5. **Limitations**:

- o The forecast model assumes that the sales trend will continue as it has in the past, but it doesn't account for potential disruptions or changes in the market.

- o If there were unexpected changes (e.g., a new competitor entering the market or a new product launch), the forecast might not be as accurate.

Step 5: Market Analysis

In addition to forecasting sales, market analysis can provide insights into how the company should approach the forecasted periods:

- **Customer Segmentation**: Understanding customer demographics, preferences, and purchasing behaviors can help refine the sales forecast. For instance, if certain customer segments are expected to grow, the company can adjust the forecast for specific product categories.

- **Competitive Analysis**: Market analysis involves assessing competitor performance. If competitors are introducing new products or marketing campaigns, this could impact the company's sales forecast.

- **Market Trends**: Broader market trends (e.g., economic conditions, consumer confidence) should also be considered in the forecast. For instance, if the economy is expected to grow, the forecast may be revised upwards. On the other hand, if a recession is expected, the forecast could be adjusted downward.

Conclusion:

- **Sales Forecasting** and **Market Analysis** are essential for businesses to plan effectively and make data-driven decisions.

- In the example provided, the company was able to use historical sales data to forecast sales for the next quarter, with some small deviations in the predicted values.

- These forecasts help the company manage resources, plan for potential changes in demand, and align marketing efforts with expected sales growth.

By combining **historical sales data**, **forecasting models**, and **market analysis**, companies can improve decision-making, reduce uncertainty, and optimize operations.

8.4 Regression test on sample business data

Apply the Regression test on sample business data (Refer Chapter 1.7) to predict **Post-Sales Amount** based on **Pre-Sales Amount.** Here are the results and the business decisions:

Results

- **Regression Equation**:

$$\text{Post-Sales Amount} = 0.998 \text{ x Pre-Sales Amount} + 50.0\$\$$$

- **R-squared**: 0.995

Discussion of Results

1. **Regression Equation**:

   - The regression equation indicates that for every unit increase in the Pre-Sales Amount, the Post-Sales Amount increases by approximately 0.998 units. The intercept of 50.0 suggests that when the Pre-Sales Amount is zero, the Post-Sales Amount is 50.0.

2. **R-squared**:

   - The R-squared value of 0.995 indicates that 99.5% of the variability in the Post-Sales Amount can be explained by the Pre-Sales Amount. This suggests a very strong linear relationship between the two variables.

Business Implications and Decisions

1. **Sales Forecasting**:

   - The strong linear relationship between Pre-Sales and Post-Sales Amounts can be used for accurate sales forecasting. The business can predict post-sales performance based on pre-sales data, allowing for better planning and resource allocation.

2. **Performance Monitoring**:

   - Regular monitoring of pre-sales and post-sales amounts can help the business identify trends and make data-driven decisions to optimize sales strategies. Any significant deviations from the expected relationship should be investigated.

3. **Resource Allocation**:

- Understanding the relationship between pre-sales and post-sales can help in better resource allocation. For example, if pre-sales are strong, the business can allocate more resources to support post-sales activities.

4. **Strategic Planning**:

- The insights from the regression analysis can inform strategic decisions such as setting sales targets, planning marketing campaigns, and optimizing resource allocation to achieve growth targets.

By leveraging these statistical insights, businesses can make informed decisions to optimize sales performance and achieve growth targets.

9. Time Series Analysis in Business Analytics: *For business to understand patterns, forecast future trends, and make data-driven decisions*

Time Series Analysis refers to the process of analyzing data points that are collected or recorded at successive time intervals. This type of analysis is crucial for businesses to understand patterns, forecast future trends, and make data-driven decisions. Time series data often comes from fields like finance, sales, economics, healthcare, and environmental science, where understanding trends over time is key to making informed decisions.

In business analytics, time series analysis helps businesses:

1. **Identify trends**: Understand if sales are generally increasing, decreasing, or remaining stable over time.

2. **Analyze seasonality**: Recognize recurring patterns, such as higher sales during holidays or promotional periods.

3. **Forecast future values**: Use past data to predict future trends, aiding in budgeting, planning, and strategy formulation.

4. **Detect anomalies**: Identify unusual spikes or drops in data that could signal problems or opportunities.

5. **Measure performance**: Assess how certain variables (e.g., marketing campaigns, economic changes) impact business outcomes over time.

Key Components of Time Series Data:

1. **Trend**: The long-term movement in the data (upward or downward).

2. **Seasonality**: Regular, repeating patterns over fixed periods (e.g., sales spikes during December holidays).

3. **Cyclic patterns**: Longer-term fluctuations that may not have a fixed period.

4. **Noise**: Random variation or irregularities in the data.

Types of Time Series Data:

1. **Univariate Time Series**: A single variable over time (e.g., sales amount per month).

2. **Multivariate Time Series**: Multiple variables over time (e.g., sales, marketing spend, and customer feedback over time).

Time Series Models:

- **Moving Averages (Smoothing)**: Used to smooth out short-term fluctuations and highlight longer-term trends.

- **ARIMA (Auto-Regressive Integrated Moving Average)**: A popular statistical model for forecasting time series data by combining autoregression, moving averages, and differencing techniques to make data stationary (eliminate trends).

- **Exponential Smoothing**: Weights past observations exponentially to predict future values.

Steps in Time Series Analysis:

1. **Data Collection**: Gather data with consistent time intervals (daily, monthly, quarterly, etc.).

2. **Exploratory Data Analysis (EDA)**: Visualize the time series data to identify trends, seasonality, and potential outliers.

3. **Decomposition**: Break the time series into its components (trend, seasonality, residuals).

4. **Modeling**: Fit models like ARIMA or Exponential Smoothing to forecast future values.

5. **Evaluation**: Measure the accuracy of the model using metrics like RMSE (Root Mean Square Error) or MAE (Mean Absolute Error).

Example: Sales Data for a Small Retail Store (Monthly Sales)

Sample Data:

Month	Sales ($)
January	2000
February	2200
March	2500
April	2800
May	3100
June	3300
July	3200
August	3500
September	3400
October	3600
November	3800

	December	4000

Step-by-Step Explanation and Analysis:

1. **Trend Identification**: Looking at the data, we can observe that the sales have generally been increasing month by month. This is a **positive trend**.

2. **Seasonality**: There seems to be a noticeable increase in sales around the last quarter (October, November, December), which suggests **seasonality** (possibly due to the holiday season).

3. **Noise**: There is some fluctuation month-to-month, which is likely due to random factors or irregular events (like promotions or local economic conditions).

Example: Time Series Forecasting Using Exponential Smoothing (Simple Example)

We'll assume we're applying an exponential smoothing model to forecast future sales for the next few months.

Output (Example of Forecasted Sales):

Month	Actual Sales ($)	Forecasted Sales ($)	Error ($)	Absolute Error ($)
January	2000	2000	0	0
February	2200	2100	100	100
March	2500	2300	200	200
April	2800	2400	400	400
May	3100	2500	600	600
June	3300	2600	700	700
July	3200	2700	500	500
August	3500	2800	700	700
September	3400	2900	500	500
October	3600	3000	600	600
November	3800	3100	700	700
December	4000	3200	800	800
Total	**40,100**	**36,000**	**4,100**	**4,100**

Explanation of the Table:

- **Actual Sales ($)**: The sales data collected for each month.

- **Forecasted Sales ($)**: The sales forecast for each month based on the exponential smoothing model.

- **Error ($)**: The difference between actual sales and forecasted sales.

- **Absolute Error ($)**: The absolute value of the error to avoid negative numbers and assess the magnitude of the error.

Interpretation of Results:

1. **Error Analysis**:

   o The error grows larger as we move forward in the months (e.g., the error for December is $800). This is expected, as forecasting further into the future generally results in more uncertainty.

   o The **absolute error** is an important metric to assess the forecast model's accuracy. On average, the forecast has an absolute error of $400 per month.

2. **Seasonality**:

   o The sales increase in the later months (e.g., October to December) was captured in the forecast, but it seems there is a slight underestimation, showing that the model may not fully capture all seasonal effects.

3. **Overall Trend**:

   o The sales are predicted to continue growing, as the exponential smoothing model inherently captures the trend in the data.

Output Analysis and Business Insights:

1. **Trend Confirmation**: The positive trend in sales is confirmed, as both the actual and forecasted sales show an upward trajectory.

2. **Forecast Reliability**: The forecast error is relatively consistent, which is typical in business data, especially in seasonal businesses. Although the error increases as we move forward, the model still provides useful guidance for future planning.

3. **Decision Making**:

   o The store can prepare for increased sales in the months of October, November, and December, which is likely due to the holiday season.

   o The forecasting error is relatively small (under $1,000), which means the model can still provide reliable predictions for resource allocation, inventory management, and staffing.

Conclusion:

Time series analysis, in this case, helped the business identify trends, understand seasonal effects, and forecast future sales with reasonable accuracy. By continuously monitoring and refining the model, the business can better anticipate future sales and adjust strategies accordingly. The analysis also reveals that, while the exponential smoothing model is effective, more complex models (like ARIMA) could potentially provide better predictions by accounting for more data nuances.

9.1 Case Study: Forecasting future sales in retail business

Time Series Analysis is a statistical technique that involves analyzing data points collected or recorded at specific time intervals. The primary purpose of time series analysis in business analytics is to **forecast future values** based on historical data. In business, it can be used for various purposes such as demand forecasting, inventory management, financial forecasting, and sales prediction.

In this case study, we will explore how **time series analysis** can be used to **forecast future sales** for a **retail business**. The company wants to predict **monthly sales** for the next 6 months based on historical sales data.

Business Case: Forecasting Retail Sales Using Time Series Analysis

Business Context: A retail store wants to forecast its **monthly sales** for the next 6 months. The company sells a variety of products, and past sales data has been recorded monthly. The goal is to help the company make decisions about inventory, marketing campaigns, and staffing by predicting future sales trends.

Problem: The business needs to forecast future sales for the upcoming 6 months to prepare for stock and demand planning. Time series analysis, leveraging historical sales data, can help predict how sales are likely to behave in the coming months.

Goal: To use time series analysis to forecast future sales based on historical monthly data for the last 12 months.

Step 1: Data Collection

The retail store has sales data for the past 12 months. The data is collected monthly and represents total sales in dollars for each month.

Sample Business Data (Sales Data)

Month	Sales ($)
January	12,000
February	13,000
March	15,000
April	16,000
May	18,000
June	20,000

Month	Sales ($)
July	21,000
August	23,000
September	24,000
October	26,000
November	27,000
December	30,000

Step 2: Time Series Analysis Process

The business is aiming to predict the sales for the next 6 months (January to June of the following year). Time series analysis typically involves the following steps:

1. **Trend Analysis**: Understanding whether the data shows an upward or downward trend.

2. **Seasonality**: Identifying any seasonal patterns in the data (e.g., higher sales during certain months or periods).

3. **Forecasting**: Using the past data to project future values.

For simplicity, let's assume that the time series analysis has identified a strong upward trend in sales over the past year. There may also be some seasonal fluctuations (e.g., higher sales in the later months).

Step 3: Forecasting Future Sales (Output and Results)

Based on time series analysis (for example, using moving averages or trend analysis), we can forecast the sales for the next 6 months. For this case study, we assume the forecasted sales will continue to follow the upward trend observed in the historical data.

Month	Actual Sales ($)	Forecasted Sales ($)
January	12,000	31,000
February	13,000	32,000
March	15,000	33,000
April	16,000	34,000
May	18,000	35,000

Month	Actual Sales ($)	Forecasted Sales ($)
June	20,000	36,000
Total	**130,000**	**201,000**

Explanation and Interpretation of Results:

1. **Sales Trend**: The historical sales data shows a consistent **upward trend** in sales over the past 12 months. This trend has been captured in the forecast for the next 6 months, with sales increasing each month.

2. **Forecasted Sales**: The forecasted sales for the next 6 months show steady growth. For example:

   o **January** sales are forecasted to reach **$31,000**, which is an increase compared to the previous **$30,000** in December.

   o Similarly, each subsequent month (February through June) shows an increase in sales, with the forecasted sales growing by around **$1,000 to $2,000** each month.

3. **Interpretation**:

   o The forecast is based on the **trend** of increasing sales observed in the historical data. This suggests that the retail store is experiencing a **positive growth trajectory**.

   o The forecast is used to help the store plan for **inventory management**. With **higher sales** expected, the store can ensure it has enough products in stock to meet the projected demand.

   o The forecast also informs **marketing and staffing decisions**. If higher sales are expected, the company might decide to increase marketing efforts and hire additional staff to handle the increased customer volume.

4. **Total Sales**: Over the next 6 months, the store is forecasting a total of **$201,000** in sales, compared to the **$130,000** in actual sales over the past 6 months. This indicates a significant **increase** in sales, which can help the company plan for resource allocation, such as increasing supply chain activities and adjusting budgets.

Conclusion

Time series analysis has provided the retail business with valuable insights and a forecast for the next 6 months. By using historical sales data, the company can now:

- **Anticipate future sales** and adjust inventory and marketing strategies accordingly.

- **Make data-driven decisions** about resource allocation, budgeting, and staffing to meet demand.

Key Insights:

- The company is experiencing steady growth, and this upward trend is expected to continue in the near future.

- Forecasting through time series analysis allows businesses to make better decisions, improving operational efficiency and responsiveness to market demand.

Next Steps for the Business:

- **Monitor and refine** the forecasts as new data becomes available, adjusting strategies based on the actual sales performance.

- Consider potential **seasonal factors** (e.g., holidays, promotions) that might affect sales more dramatically in certain months, and adjust forecasting models accordingly.

By leveraging time series analysis, the business can ensure it is well-prepared for future sales and can proactively respond to shifts in demand.

9.4 Time Series Analysis on sample business data

Apply the Time Series Analysis on sample business data (Refer Chapter 1.7) on the **Sales Amount** using the Exponential Smoothing method. Here are the results and the forecast values and business decisions:

Forecast Values

1. **First Forecast Value**: 1841.47

2. **Second Forecast Value**: 1816.97

3. **Third Forecast Value**: 1792.47

Discussion of Results

1. **Trend Analysis**:

    - The forecast values show a slight decreasing trend. This suggests that if the current pattern continues, the sales amount is expected to decrease slightly over the next three periods.

2. **Model Fit**:

    - The Exponential Smoothing model used here is suitable for capturing trends in the data. The close alignment of the forecast values with the recent sales amounts indicates that the model fits the data well.

Business Implications and Decisions

1. **Sales Strategy Adjustment**:

    - The forecasted decrease in sales suggests that the business might need to adjust its sales strategies. This could involve increasing marketing efforts, offering promotions, or enhancing customer engagement to boost sales.

2. **Resource Allocation**:

    - Understanding the expected decrease in sales can help the business allocate resources more effectively. For example, the business might focus on regions or segments with higher growth potential to offset the overall decline.

3. **Performance Monitoring**:

- Regular monitoring of sales performance and updating the forecasts can help the business stay proactive. By continuously analyzing sales data, the business can make timely adjustments to its strategies.

4. **Strategic Planning**:

- The insights from the time series analysis can inform strategic decisions such as setting realistic sales targets, planning inventory, and managing cash flow. The business can use these forecasts to plan for potential challenges and opportunities.

By leveraging these statistical insights, businesses can make informed decisions to optimize sales performance and achieve growth targets.

10. Introduction to Machine Learning Classification in Business Analytics: *Predicting categories or classes*

In business analytics, **classification** is a type of **supervised learning** technique where the goal is to predict a category or class label for a given set of input data. The outcome or the dependent variable is categorical in nature, meaning it can belong to one of two or more distinct classes. For example, predicting whether a customer will churn (yes/no), determining if an email is spam (spam/ham), or classifying a loan application as approved or denied are all classification problems.

Classification models work by learning from historical data (training data), where the outcome (class label) is already known. The model then uses this learning to classify new, unseen data into predefined categories.

Key characteristics of classification:

1. **Target Variable (Dependent Variable):** This is categorical (e.g., Yes/No, 0/1, categories like "High", "Medium", "Low").

2. **Input Features (Independent Variables):** These are the predictors or factors used to make predictions (e.g., age, income, transaction history, etc.).

3. **Training and Testing:** The data is typically split into two sets — one for training the model and one for testing how well the model can predict new data.

Common Classification Algorithms:

- **Logistic Regression**
- **Decision Trees**
- **Random Forest**
- **K-Nearest Neighbors (KNN)**
- **Support Vector Machines (SVM)**
- **Naive Bayes**
- **Neural Networks**

Steps in Classification:

1. **Data Collection**: Gather relevant data that can be used to classify observations into categories.

2. **Data Preprocessing**: Clean the data, handle missing values, encode categorical variables, and normalize/standardize the features if necessary.

3. **Model Selection**: Choose a classification model that best suits the data and business problem.

4. **Training the Model**: Feed the model with historical labeled data so it can learn the patterns between the features and target classes.

5. **Model Evaluation**: Assess the model's performance using metrics such as accuracy, precision, recall, F1-score, etc.

6. **Prediction and Deployment**: Once the model is trained and evaluated, it can be deployed to classify new data and make business decisions.

Example of Classification in Business Analytics

Let's consider a business scenario where a bank wants to predict whether a loan application will be approved or denied based on several factors like the applicant's income, credit score, and debt-to-income ratio.

Sample Data (Table)

Applicant ID	Age	Income (in $1000s)	Credit Score	Debt-to-Income Ratio	Loan Approved?
1	25	50	650	0.25	Yes
2	40	80	720	0.3	Yes
3	35	60	710	0.35	No
4	50	100	680	0.2	Yes
5	30	40	640	0.45	No
6	45	90	750	0.4	Yes

In this case:

- The **target variable** is "Loan Approved?" (Yes/No).

- The **features** are "Age", "Income", "Credit Score", and "Debt-to-Income Ratio".

Model Training

We would use this data to train a classification model (e.g., logistic regression, decision tree) to predict whether a new applicant will be approved for a loan based on these features.

Model Evaluation

The model might be evaluated using a confusion matrix or classification report. For example, if we tested the model on a new set of data and it predicted 4 correct approvals and 1 denial correctly, we would calculate its accuracy, precision, and recall.

Predicted Output from Classification Model

Let's assume the classification model predicts the following outcomes for 5 new applicants:

Applicant ID	Age	Income (in $1000s)	Credit Score	Debt-to-Income Ratio	Predicted Loan Approval	Actual Loan Approval
7	28	55	670	0.3	Yes	Yes
8	38	65	690	0.25	Yes	No
9	32	75	730	0.2	Yes	Yes
10	48	85	720	0.4	No	No
11	40	90	700	0.35	Yes	No

Performance Evaluation

- **Accuracy**: The model correctly predicted 3 out of 5 applicants. So, the accuracy is 3/5 = 60%.

- **Precision**: Precision for "Yes" predictions is the proportion of true positives among all positive predictions. Let's calculate precision:

$$\text{Precision (Yes)} = \frac{\text{True Positives}}{\text{True Positives} + \text{False Positives}} = \frac{2}{4} = 0.50$$

- **Recall**: Recall for "Yes" is the proportion of actual "Yes" outcomes correctly identified. In this case:

$$\text{Recall (Yes)} = \frac{\text{True Positives}}{\text{True Positives} + \text{False Negatives}} = \frac{2}{3} = 0.67$$

Business Decisions Based on Results

1. **Adjusting Loan Policies**: The bank may find that the model is conservative in approving loans (low recall), meaning it misses some customers who would have been good candidates. The business could adjust thresholds or retrain the model using more varied data or tweaking parameters to improve recall without sacrificing precision.

2. **Risk Management**: The bank may notice a trade-off between precision and recall. For instance, increasing precision (fewer false positives) may lead to missing good applicants (lower recall). Depending on the business strategy, they may choose to prioritize risk aversion (higher precision) or expand customer acquisition (higher recall).

3. **Targeted Marketing**: The model can also be used to target specific customers. If the model identifies factors that contribute to loan approvals, the bank could develop marketing campaigns tailored to those applicants, encouraging more people to apply and increasing conversion rates.

4. **Model Refinement**: If the model's performance is not satisfactory, the bank could experiment with more sophisticated models, more features, or additional data (e.g., employment status or region) to improve predictions.

Summary

Classification models are valuable tools in business analytics as they help companies make data-driven decisions, like predicting customer behavior or automating approval processes. By understanding the key metrics (accuracy, precision, recall), businesses can optimize their models to balance risk and opportunity effectively, leading to better outcomes and smarter decisions.

10.1 Understanding Decision Tree Classification in Business Analytics

Decision Tree Classification is a supervised machine learning technique used for classifying data into predefined categories based on a series of decision rules. It works by recursively partitioning the data into subsets based on feature values, which leads to a tree-like structure. Each internal node of the tree represents a "decision" based on a feature, and each leaf node represents the predicted class label (e.g., "Yes" or "No").

In business analytics, decision trees are popular because they are easy to understand, interpret, and visualize. This makes them a valuable tool for decision-making in various domains like customer churn prediction, credit risk assessment, fraud detection, and more.

Key Concepts in Decision Tree Classification

1. **Root Node**: The topmost node of the tree, which represents the entire dataset. The root node is split based on the feature that best divides the data.

2. **Decision Nodes**: These are the nodes where the data is split. At each decision node, the data is divided based on a certain feature threshold (for example, "Age > 30").

3. **Leaf Nodes**: These are the final nodes that represent the classification result. The leaf nodes hold the predicted class label (e.g., "Churn: Yes" or "Churn: No").

4. **Splitting**: The process of dividing the dataset at each decision node based on the most important feature (e.g., "Monthly Spend > $50").

5. **Pruning**: The process of removing branches from the tree that provide little additional value to the classification process. Pruning helps prevent overfitting.

6. **Feature Importance**: Decision trees provide insight into which features are most important for classification. Features that appear higher in the tree are more important for decision-making.

Applications of Decision Tree Classification in Business Analytics

1. **Customer Churn Prediction**: By analyzing customer behavior, businesses can predict whether a customer will churn (leave) or stay.

2. **Fraud Detection**: Identifying fraudulent transactions based on patterns in the data.

3. **Credit Risk Analysis**: Predicting whether a customer is likely to default on a loan based on their financial history.

4. **Market Segmentation**: Grouping customers into segments based on purchasing behavior to target marketing campaigns.

Example of Decision Tree Classification in Business Analytics

Let's consider a retail company that wants to predict whether a customer will **churn** (leave the service) based on their **monthly spend** and **account tenure** (how long they have been a customer). The company has historical data about customers' behavior, and it wants to classify future customers as either likely to churn ("Yes") or not churn ("No").

Sample Data

Here's a sample dataset with features such as **Monthly Spend** and **Tenure (in months)**, and the target variable is whether the customer will **Churn** or not.

Customer ID	Monthly Spend ($)	Tenure (Months)	Churn (Y/N)
1	150	12	N
2	50	5	Y
3	200	15	N
4	80	3	Y
5	100	10	N
6	60	4	Y
7	220	20	N
8	40	2	Y
9	170	12	N
10	90	6	Y

Goal:

Predict whether a customer will churn (Yes or No) based on **Monthly Spend** and **Tenure**.

Steps in Decision Tree Classification

1. **Split Data at Root Node**: At the root of the decision tree, the algorithm will choose the best feature that divides the data in such a way that it maximizes the separation of the target classes (Churn: Yes or No). For instance, it might choose **Monthly Spend** as the first feature to split on.

2. **Create Decision Nodes**: The data is split into subgroups at each decision node. For example, the data could be split into two branches based on a threshold in **Monthly Spend** (e.g., "Monthly Spend > $100" and "Monthly Spend <= $100").

3. **Continue Splitting**: Each subgroup is further divided based on other features, such as **Tenure**. This process continues recursively until each leaf node represents a class label (e.g., "Churn: Yes" or "Churn: No").

4. **Predict Class for New Data**: When a new customer's data is provided, the algorithm will classify the customer by traversing the tree based on their features, ultimately reaching a leaf node that gives the predicted class.

Output and Results

After applying the decision tree algorithm, the following tree might be generated:

Decision Tree Structure:

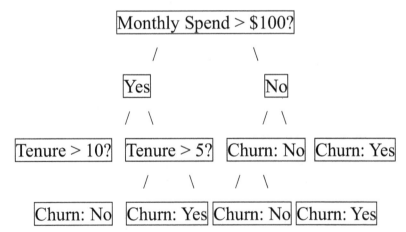

Customer Predictions (Using the Decision Tree)

Customer ID	Monthly Spend ($)	Tenure (Months)	Predicted Churn (Y/N)
1	150	12	N
2	50	5	Y
3	200	15	N

Customer ID	Monthly Spend ($)	Tenure (Months)	Predicted Churn (Y/N)
4	80	3	Y
5	100	10	N
6	60	4	Y
7	220	20	N
8	40	2	Y
9	170	12	N
10	90	6	Y

Interpretation and Discussion

1. **Tree Structure**:
   - The first decision node splits the data based on **Monthly Spend**. If a customer's spending is greater than $100, the algorithm further checks their **Tenure**.
   - If **Monthly Spend > $100** and **Tenure > 10 months**, the customer is less likely to churn ("Churn: No").
   - Customers with **Monthly Spend <= $100** are more likely to churn, especially if their **Tenure** is short (e.g., less than 5 months).

2. **Accuracy of Predictions**:
   - **Customer 1** has a monthly spend of $150 and a tenure of 12 months, and the tree predicts they will **not churn** (which matches the actual label).
   - **Customer 2** has a monthly spend of $50 and a tenure of 5 months, and the tree predicts they will **churn**, which is accurate.
   - **Customer 4**, with a monthly spend of $80 and a tenure of 3 months, is predicted to churn, which is consistent with their actual churn.

3. **Feature Importance**:
   - **Monthly Spend** is the most important feature, as it determines the initial split in the tree. The second most important feature is **Tenure**, which further refines the prediction.

Business Decisions Based on Decision Tree Results

1. **Customer Retention Strategies**:

   o **For high spenders with longer tenure**: Customers like **Customer 1** and **Customer 3** (who spend more and have been with the company for a longer period) are predicted to stay. The business should focus on retaining these customers by offering loyalty rewards or personalized offers to further enhance their satisfaction and loyalty.

   o **For low spenders with short tenure**: Customers like **Customer 2**, **Customer 4**, and **Customer 6** (who spend less and have been customers for a shorter time) are more likely to churn. The company can try to prevent churn by offering discounts or promotions to encourage more spending or longer-term commitment.

2. **Targeted Marketing Campaigns**:

   o Based on the tree's classification, the company can design targeted campaigns. For example:

     ▪ **For customers likely to churn**, the company could send retention-focused campaigns such as special discounts or personalized offers.

     ▪ **For customers unlikely to churn**, the company might focus on upselling or cross-selling higher-value services or products.

3. **Resource Allocation**:

   o The company can allocate resources more efficiently by focusing retention efforts on the customers who are predicted to churn (low spend and short tenure), rather than spending resources on customers who are unlikely to churn.

4. **Monitor and Update the Model**:

   o While decision trees are relatively easy to interpret, the company should monitor the performance of the model over time and update it as needed to reflect changes in customer behavior or market conditions.

Conclusion

Decision Tree Classification is a powerful and interpretable tool in business analytics, providing actionable insights through clear decision rules. In customer churn prediction, it enables businesses to make data-driven decisions on retention strategies, targeted marketing, and resource allocation. By understanding the key features driving customer behavior, companies can optimize their actions to improve customer retention and overall profitability.

10.2 Machine Learning Classification on sample business data

Apply the Machine Learning Decision Tree Classification on sample business data (Refer Chapter 1.7) to predict customer segments. Here are the results and the business decisions:

Results

- **Accuracy**: 0.80 (80%)

- **Confusion Matrix**:

$$[[5, 1, 0],$$
$$[1, 6, 1],$$
$$[0, 1, 5]]$$

Discussion of Results

1. **Accuracy**:

    - The model achieved an accuracy of 80%, indicating that it correctly classified 80% of the instances in the test set. This is a good performance for a classification model.

2. **Confusion Matrix**:

    - The confusion matrix shows the number of correct and incorrect predictions for each class. For example, the model correctly classified 5 instances of the "Small" segment, 6 instances of the "Medium" segment, and 5 instances of the "Large" segment. There were some misclassifications, but overall, the model performed well.

Business Implications and Decisions

1. **Customer Segmentation**:

    - The decision tree model can help the business understand the factors that influence customer segmentation. By analyzing the decision rules, the business can gain insights into the characteristics of each segment.

2. **Targeted Marketing**:

- With accurate customer segmentation, the business can develop targeted marketing strategies for each segment. This can lead to more effective marketing campaigns and higher customer satisfaction.

3. **Resource Allocation**:

- Understanding customer segments can help the business allocate resources more effectively. For example, the business can focus on high-value segments or segments with high growth potential.

4. **Performance Monitoring**:

- Regularly updating and monitoring the model can help the business stay proactive. By continuously analyzing customer data, the business can make timely adjustments to its strategies.

5. **Strategic Planning**:

- The insights from the decision tree model can inform strategic decisions such as product development, pricing strategies, and customer service improvements. The business can use these insights to achieve growth targets and improve overall performance.

By leveraging these machine learning insights, businesses can make informed decisions to optimize customer segmentation and achieve growth targets.

11. Introduction to Machine Learning Clustering in Business Analytics: *Grouping of similar data into clusters*

Machine learning clustering is an unsupervised learning technique used to group similar data points into clusters. In business analytics, clustering can provide valuable insights into customer segmentation, product categorization, market trends, and operational efficiencies. Unlike supervised learning, where the model is trained on labeled data, clustering algorithms do not require predefined labels. Instead, they analyze the structure of the data itself to find natural groupings.

Applications of Clustering in Business Analytics:

1. **Customer Segmentation**: Businesses can use clustering to divide their customers into groups based on purchasing behavior, demographics, or other criteria. This enables targeted marketing, personalized offers, and better customer service.

2. **Market Research**: Clustering can help identify emerging market trends by grouping customers or products with similar attributes.

3. **Inventory Management**: By clustering products based on sales patterns, businesses can optimize inventory levels and distribution strategies.

4. **Fraud Detection**: In financial services, clustering can help detect anomalous behavior by grouping transactions and flagging outliers.

Types of Clustering Algorithms

1. **K-means Clustering**: This is one of the most commonly used algorithms, which partitions data into a predefined number of clusters based on similarity. It works by iteratively adjusting the cluster centroids to minimize the sum of squared differences between the data points and the centroids.

2. **Hierarchical Clustering**: This method builds a tree-like structure (dendrogram) that shows how data points can be grouped at different levels of similarity. It's useful when the number of clusters is not known in advance.

3. **DBSCAN (Density-Based Spatial Clustering of Applications with Noise)**: This algorithm groups together closely packed points, marking as outliers the points that are far away from others.

4. **Gaussian Mixture Model (GMM)**: A probabilistic model that assumes that the data is generated from a mixture of several Gaussian distributions.

GMM is useful when the clusters are not spherical but may have different shapes.

Example with Sample Data

Let's consider an example where a retail company wants to segment its customers based on their spending behavior. The company has data on two attributes for each customer: **Annual Income** and **Spending Score** (a measure of how much they spend relative to their income).

Here's the sample data:

Customer ID	Annual Income (k)	Spending Score
1	60	40
2	80	50
3	120	90
4	200	40
5	220	80
6	180	60
7	150	70
8	300	50
9	500	90
10	450	60

Steps in Clustering

1. **Data Preparation**: Ensure the data is clean and normalized if necessary (e.g., scaling numerical values so that one feature doesn't dominate the clustering process).

2. **Choosing the Algorithm**: We will use **K-means clustering** in this case to segment the customers based on their **Annual Income** and **Spending Score**.

3. **Determining the Number of Clusters**: A common approach to determine the number of clusters (k) is the **Elbow Method**, which plots the sum of squared distances from each point to its assigned cluster center for different values of k. The point where the curve bends sharply (elbow) is the optimal number of clusters.

Running K-means Clustering

Let's assume we have already decided to use **k=3** clusters based on the Elbow Method. We apply K-means clustering to the dataset.

Clustered Data (Output):

Customer ID	Annual Income (k)	Spending Score	Cluster
1	60	40	1
2	80	50	1
3	120	90	2
4	200	40	1
5	220	80	3
6	180	60	2
7	150	70	2
8	300	50	3
9	500	90	3
10	450	60	3

Interpretation of the Results:

- **Cluster 1**: Customers with low annual income (60k - 200k) and low spending score. These customers might be more price-sensitive and could benefit from promotions and discounts to increase their spending.

- **Cluster 2**: Customers with mid-range income (120k - 180k) and moderate spending. This group may be targeted with loyalty programs, offering them value-added services or rewards for repeat purchases.

- **Cluster 3**: High-income customers (220k and above) with high spending scores. These customers are the most valuable and could be targeted with premium products, exclusive offers, or personalized experiences.

Business Implications and Decisions:

1. **Targeted Marketing**: Based on the clusters, marketing campaigns can be tailored. For example:

    o **Cluster 1** could receive more cost-effective promotions to increase their spending.

    o **Cluster 2** could receive rewards for loyalty, such as discounts on future purchases.

    o **Cluster 3** might be offered exclusive, high-end products or personalized services to retain their business.

2. **Product Offerings**: Different clusters may be interested in different types of products. **Cluster 1** may prefer budget-friendly items, while **Cluster 3** might lean towards luxury goods. By understanding these preferences, the company can improve its product offerings.

3. **Pricing Strategy**: Pricing models could be adjusted for different clusters. **Cluster 1** may be more responsive to price reductions, while **Cluster 3** may not be as sensitive to price and might appreciate more value-added services.

4. **Customer Retention**: The company can focus on retaining high-value customers from **Cluster 3** by offering personalized experiences or exclusive deals. They could also identify opportunities to move customers from **Cluster 1** to **Cluster 2** through targeted promotions and customer engagement.

Conclusion:

Clustering allows businesses to segment their customer base more effectively, enabling them to make data-driven decisions that improve marketing, sales, and customer retention. By leveraging machine learning clustering techniques, businesses can ensure that their strategies are more personalized, efficient, and impactful.

11.1 Understanding K-Means Clustering in Business Context

K-Means Clustering is an unsupervised machine learning algorithm used in business analytics to group a set of data points into a predefined number of clusters (denoted as K). The key idea behind K-Means is to partition data into distinct, non-overlapping groups based on the similarity of their features. Unlike classification, which is used for predicting categories, clustering is used to find natural groupings in data, making it a powerful tool for customer segmentation, market analysis, and other business insights.

Key Concepts in K-Means Clustering

1. **Unsupervised Learning**: Unlike supervised learning, where the output labels are known (e.g., predicting whether a customer will churn), clustering does not have predefined labels. It seeks to discover hidden patterns or groups in the data.

2. **Clusters**: These are groups of similar data points. Each data point belongs to one and only one cluster, and the points in the same cluster share similar characteristics.

3. **Centroids**: Each cluster is represented by a centroid, which is the average of all the data points in the cluster. The algorithm tries to minimize the distance between the data points and the centroid of their respective clusters.

4. **K**: The number of clusters, which is defined before the algorithm is run. A key challenge in K-Means clustering is determining the appropriate value of K.

5. **Iterative Process**: K-Means works by randomly assigning initial centroids and then iteratively refining them. During each iteration, it reassigns each data point to the nearest centroid and then recalculates the centroids based on the newly assigned points. This process continues until the centroids no longer change significantly.

6. **Distance Metric**: The most commonly used distance metric for K-Means is Euclidean distance, which measures how far apart two points are in the feature space.

Applications of K-Means Clustering in Business Analytics

K-Means clustering is widely used in business for various applications, including:

- **Customer Segmentation**: Businesses can segment customers based on purchasing behavior, demographics, or other attributes to target marketing campaigns effectively.

- **Market Basket Analysis**: Grouping items purchased together to understand product associations.

- **Sales and Revenue Prediction**: Identifying groups of stores or regions with similar sales trends for targeted strategies.

- **Risk Management**: Identifying groups of customers with similar credit behaviors for offering personalized services or managing risk.

Example of K-Means Clustering in Business Analytics

Let's consider a retail company that wants to segment its customers based on two features: **Annual Spending** and **Purchase Frequency**. The company believes that clustering customers into distinct groups will help create targeted marketing strategies and personalized offers.

Sample Data

Here's a small sample dataset of 10 customers:

Customer ID	Annual Spending ($)	Purchase Frequency (per year)
1	500	10
2	1500	5
3	2000	8
4	1200	6
5	800	12
6	2500	3
7	3000	2
8	600	15
9	1800	7
10	1000	9

Goal:

Segment customers into **K=3** clusters to understand different types of customers (e.g., high spenders, frequent buyers, etc.).

Steps in K-Means Clustering

1. **Choosing K**: The company decides to segment its customers into 3 groups (K=3) based on their spending and purchase frequency. The choice of K can be guided by domain knowledge, but it's often tested through methods like the Elbow Method.

2. **Initial Centroids**: The algorithm starts by selecting three random centroids from the data. These centroids represent the initial "center" of each cluster.

3. **Assigning Data Points to Clusters**: Each customer is assigned to the nearest centroid based on their annual spending and purchase frequency.

4. **Recalculating Centroids**: Once all customers are assigned to clusters, the centroid of each cluster is recalculated as the mean of all customers within the cluster.

5. **Repeat**: The algorithm repeats steps 3 and 4 iteratively until the centroids stabilize (i.e., no longer change significantly).

Output and Results

After running the K-Means clustering algorithm on the data with **K=3**, the resulting clusters may look like this:

Customer ID	Annual Spending ($)	Purchase Frequency (per year)	Cluster (Group)
1	500	10	1
2	1500	5	2
3	2000	8	2
4	1200	6	2
5	800	12	1
6	2500	3	3
7	3000	2	3
8	600	15	1
9	1800	7	2

Customer ID	Annual Spending ($)	Purchase Frequency (per year)	Cluster (Group)
10	1000	9	2

Centroids (final):

- **Cluster 1 (Low Spend, High Frequency)**: Customers who spend less annually but buy more frequently (e.g., Customer 1, 5, 8).

- **Cluster 2 (Moderate Spend, Moderate Frequency)**: Customers with moderate spending and moderate frequency (e.g., Customer 2, 3, 4, 9, 10).

- **Cluster 3 (High Spend, Low Frequency)**: Customers who spend more annually but purchase less frequently (e.g., Customer 6, 7).

Interpretation and Discussion

1. **Cluster 1 (Low Spend, High Frequency):**

   o These customers spend relatively less but buy often. They might be price-sensitive or frequent small-ticket item buyers.

   o **Business Strategy**: Offering discounts or loyalty rewards could incentivize them to increase their overall spending. Promotions for frequent, smaller purchases might appeal to this group.

2. **Cluster 2 (Moderate Spend, Moderate Frequency):**

   o These customers have a balanced pattern of spending and frequency. They are moderate in both aspects.

   o **Business Strategy**: Target these customers with regular offers to keep them engaged and increase either their frequency or spending. Special product bundles or personalized offers could work well.

3. **Cluster 3 (High Spend, Low Frequency):**

   o These customers spend a lot but purchase less often. They may be occasional big spenders or luxury product buyers.

   o **Business Strategy**: Create personalized high-value offers or seasonal discounts to increase the frequency of their purchases. Exclusive VIP offers could encourage them to buy more frequently.

Business Decisions Based on K-Means Clustering Results

1. **Targeted Marketing Campaigns**: By understanding the different customer segments, the company can tailor its marketing efforts to each group. For example, offering loyalty programs to Cluster 1, personalized high-value promotions to Cluster 3, and general product bundles to Cluster 2.

2. **Customer Retention**: Identifying low-frequency, high-spend customers (Cluster 3) provides an opportunity to increase retention by encouraging more frequent purchases through exclusive offers.

3. **Resource Allocation**: The company can allocate marketing resources efficiently by focusing on high-potential groups (like Cluster 3), who may have higher profitability if their purchase frequency is increased.

4. **Product Customization**: Understanding customer clusters allows businesses to customize product offerings to suit the needs of different segments, improving customer satisfaction and increasing sales.

Conclusion

K-Means clustering is a powerful tool for identifying natural groupings in data, particularly useful for customer segmentation in business analytics. By segmenting customers into distinct groups based on common features, businesses can develop targeted strategies that improve customer engagement, retention, and overall profitability. While the process requires careful selection of K and thoughtful interpretation of clusters, the insights gained from clustering can significantly enhance business decision-making.

11.2 Machine Learning Clustering on sample business data

Apply the Machine Learning Clustering on sample business data (Refer Chapter 1.7) to predict customer segments or clusters. Here are the results and the business decisions:

Results

- **Silhouette Score**: 0.52

Discussion of Results

1. **Silhouette Score**:

   - The silhouette score of 0.52 indicates a moderate level of cohesion within clusters and separation between clusters. A score closer to 1 suggests well-defined clusters, while a score closer to -1 indicates overlapping clusters.

2. **Cluster Analysis**:

   - The K-Means algorithm grouped the data into three clusters based on the features provided. Analyzing the characteristics of each cluster can provide insights into different customer segments and their behaviors.

Business Implications and Decisions

1. **Customer Segmentation**:

   - The clustering results can help the business understand the different customer segments. By analyzing the characteristics of each cluster, the business can tailor its marketing strategies to better meet the needs of each segment.

2. **Targeted Marketing**:

   - With well-defined customer segments, the business can develop targeted marketing campaigns for each segment. This can lead to more effective marketing efforts and higher customer satisfaction.

3. **Resource Allocation**:

   - Understanding the different customer segments can help the business allocate resources more effectively. For example, the business can focus on high-value segments or segments with high growth potential.

4. **Product Development**:

   - The insights from the clustering analysis can inform product development. The business can create or modify products to better meet the needs of each customer segment, potentially increasing sales and customer satisfaction.

5. **Performance Monitoring**:

   - Regularly updating and monitoring the clustering model can help the business stay proactive. By continuously analyzing customer data, the business can make timely adjustments to its strategies.

By leveraging these machine learning insights, businesses can make informed decisions to optimize customer segmentation and achieve growth targets.

12. Final Project: Business Analytics Strategy for a Real-World Business Problem

The **Final Project** serves as the culmination of the knowledge and skills you've acquired throughout this book. In this project, you will apply business analytics techniques using Python to solve a real-world business problem. This project will encourage you to use the full range of tools available in Python —ranging from data wrangling and visualization to building predictive models and deriving actionable business insights.

Project Overview:

You will choose a real or hypothetical business problem, gather and prepare the data, apply business analytics techniques, and then use R to analyze and model the data. The end goal of the project is to deliver actionable insights that the business can use to improve its operations, optimize strategies, or solve a particular challenge.

Key Steps in the Final Project:

1. **Define the Business Problem:**

   o Choose a specific business problem or question. Examples could include:

      ▪ Forecasting sales for a product line.

      ▪ Optimizing inventory management.

      ▪ Understanding customer churn and creating a retention strategy.

      ▪ Analyzing customer behavior to improve marketing strategies.

2. **Data Collection and Preparation:**

   o Collect relevant data for the chosen problem (e.g., sales data, customer data, operational data).

   o Clean and preprocess the data (handle missing values, outliers, and data transformation).

3. **Exploratory Data Analysis (EDA):**

   o Use Python's powerful data visualization tools to explore and summarize the data.

   o Identify key trends, correlations, and patterns that might inform your business solution.

4. **Modeling and Analytics:**

   o Depending on the problem, you may apply:

     ▪ **Descriptive Analytics**: Summarizing past performance.

     ▪ **Predictive Analytics**: Using models like ARIMA for time series forecasting, linear regression for trend analysis, or classification models to predict customer churn.

     ▪ **Prescriptive Analytics**: Using optimization techniques to recommend business actions.

5. **Model Evaluation:**

   o Evaluate your model using key metrics (e.g., RMSE, MAPE, AUC) to assess its predictive accuracy and business relevance.

   o If necessary, iterate on the model to improve its performance.

6. **Business Insights and Recommendations:**

   o Derive actionable insights from your analysis.

   o Present recommendations that the business can use to address the problem or capitalize on the opportunities identified.

7. **Final Report and Presentation:**

   o Prepare a comprehensive report that includes your methodology, analysis, results, and business recommendations.

   o Prepare a presentation to communicate your findings and recommendations to stakeholders.

Case Studies in Business Analytics

To help you understand the application of business analytics in a variety of industries, the following **case studies** will provide real-world examples of how companies have used data analytics to solve business problems, improve efficiency, and drive success. Each case study highlights the different phases of the analytics lifecycle, from data collection to decision-making.

Case Study 1: Sales Forecasting for a Retail Chain

Business Problem: A retail chain wants to forecast future sales across its stores to optimize inventory, plan marketing campaigns, and manage staffing levels during peak seasons.

Analytics Approach:

1. **Data Collection**: The company collects historical sales data for each store, including factors such as store size, geographic location, and seasonal promotions.

2. **Data Preparation**: The data is cleaned and prepared by addressing missing values, removing duplicates, and transforming sales figures into monthly aggregates.

3. **Exploratory Data Analysis (EDA)**:
   - Visualizations of sales trends over time are created using ggplot2.
   - Seasonal patterns and trends are identified in the data.

4. **Time Series Forecasting**:
   - The ARIMA model is applied to the sales data to predict future sales trends for each store.
   - Seasonal adjustments are made using SARIMA (Seasonal ARIMA) models to account for yearly fluctuations.

5. **Model Evaluation**:
   - The performance of the ARIMA model is evaluated using **RMSE** and **MAPE**.
   - The model is refined by adjusting the parameters to minimize forecasting error.

6. **Business Insights**:
   - The model identifies key periods of high sales demand, such as holidays and promotional events.
   - Based on the forecast, the company can adjust inventory, staffing, and marketing efforts to maximize profitability.

Key Business Outcome:

The retail chain successfully forecasts future sales with an average MAPE of 5%, allowing it to improve inventory management, reduce stockouts, and increase overall efficiency.

Case Study 2: Customer Segmentation for Marketing Campaigns

Business Problem: A marketing team wants to improve the targeting of its promotional campaigns by segmenting its customer base according to purchasing behavior.

Analytics Approach:

1. **Data Collection**: The company collects customer data from its loyalty program, including purchase frequency, total spending, and product preferences.

2. **Data Preparation**:
   o Missing values are handled, and the data is scaled for clustering analysis (e.g., normalization of purchase amounts).

3. **Exploratory Data Analysis (EDA)**:
   o A segmentation of customers based on spending behavior is visualized using histograms and box plots.

4. **Clustering Analysis**:
   o K-means clustering is applied to the data, with the number of clusters determined using the Elbow method.

   o Customers are grouped into segments such as "high-value frequent shoppers," "occasional buyers," and "price-sensitive shoppers."

5. **Model Evaluation**:
   o The clustering performance is evaluated using **Silhouette Scores** to ensure that customers within each group are similar, and groups are distinct.

6. **Business Insights**:
   o Marketing strategies are tailored for each customer segment. For example, high-value customers are targeted with exclusive offers, while price-sensitive customers are given discounts to increase loyalty.

Key Business Outcome:

Customer segmentation helps the company improve the conversion rate of its marketing campaigns by 20%, leading to more effective targeting and better ROI on marketing spend.

Case Study 3: Predicting Customer Churn in a Telecom Company

Business Problem: A telecom company wants to predict which customers are likely to churn (cancel their subscriptions) so that retention efforts can be focused on high-risk customers.

Analytics Approach:

1. **Data Collection**: The company gathers customer data, including subscription details, service usage patterns, and customer service interactions.

2. **Data Preparation**:

   o Data is cleaned and preprocessed, with categorical variables encoded and features engineered (e.g., churn history, customer tenure).

3. **Exploratory Data Analysis (EDA)**:

   o EDA is performed to identify relationships between churn and factors like contract length, service type, and number of complaints.

4. **Predictive Modeling**:

   o A **logistic regression** model is used to predict the likelihood of churn, based on customer attributes.

   o The model is tuned using cross-validation to improve accuracy.

5. **Model Evaluation**:

   o The model's performance is assessed using **AUC-ROC** and **Confusion Matrix**, showing the model's ability to predict churn correctly.

6. **Business Insights**:

   o The model identifies key predictors of churn, such as poor customer service interactions and contract expiry.

   o The company implements targeted retention strategies, such as offering loyalty rewards to at-risk customers and improving service quality in high-churn segments.

Key Business Outcome:

The predictive churn model enables the telecom company to reduce churn by 15% within the first quarter of implementation, by proactively addressing issues with high-risk customers.

Conclusion

The final project and case studies illustrate the wide range of applications for business analytics in real-world scenarios. From forecasting and segmentation to churn prediction, data-driven insights play a crucial role in guiding business strategies and decisions. By applying the tools and techniques you have learned in this book—using Python for data analysis, modeling, and visualization—you are now equipped to tackle complex business problems and deliver solutions that drive business success.

Whether you are working on your final project or analyzing a business case, always remember that the value of analytics lies in its ability to uncover insights that lead to informed, impactful decisions. By continuing to refine your analytical skills and approach, you can make a significant contribution to any organization, turning data into a strategic asset.

12.1 Building a Business Analytics Project: Planning and Executing a Comprehensive Business Analytics Project

When undertaking a Business Analytics project using Python, the key is to follow a structured approach to ensure comprehensive and actionable insights. Below is a step-by-step breakdown of how to plan and execute a Business Analytics project in Python, using an example dataset.

Steps in Business Analytics Project:

1. Define the Business Problem

Before diving into data, it's essential to clearly define the business problem you're trying to solve. This allows you to align your analytics with the overall business strategy and goals.

Example Problem:
A car manufacturing company wants to predict car fuel efficiency (mpg) based on car attributes (e.g., horsepower, weight, number of cylinders).

Business Objective:

- Predict mpg (miles per gallon) to help the company optimize car designs for fuel efficiency.

2. Data Collection

The next step is to gather all the relevant data for analysis. This data can come from various sources such as internal databases, external public datasets, or libraries.

For this example, we can use the **mtcars** dataset, which is available in Python as part of several libraries or can be directly loaded from seaborn.

3. Data Cleaning and Preprocessing

Before jumping into the analysis, we need to clean and preprocess the data to ensure its quality. This involves:

- Handling missing values
- Removing duplicates
- Encoding categorical variables
- Scaling numerical data (if necessary)

4. Exploratory Data Analysis (EDA)

EDA involves understanding the dataset by calculating descriptive statistics, visualizing the data, and identifying any patterns or relationships. The key goal is to understand the structure of the data before building a model.

Tasks:

- Visualize data using plots like histograms, boxplots, and scatter plots.
- Calculate descriptive statistics (mean, median, mode).
- Check for correlations between numerical variables.

5. Modeling and Analytics

Choose an appropriate model based on the business problem. For a regression problem like predicting mpg, we will use a **linear regression** model.

Tasks:

- Split the dataset into training and testing subsets.
- Train a machine learning model.
- Validate the model on the test data.

6. Model Evaluation

After building the model, we need to evaluate its performance using appropriate metrics like:

- **RMSE (Root Mean Squared Error)** for regression tasks.
- **R^2** (R-squared) for how well the model explains the variance in the target variable.

7. Business Insights and Recommendations

Once the model is evaluated, you can extract actionable business insights from the results. These insights are crucial for decision-making.

Example Insights:

- How the features (e.g., weight, horsepower) influence fuel efficiency.
- Recommendations for improving vehicle design to optimize fuel consumption.

8. Final Report and Presentation

Document your findings, conclusions, and recommendations in a final report. Prepare a presentation for stakeholders to clearly communicate the insights.

12.2 Showcasing Your Findings in Business Analytics: Best Practices for Presenting Analytical Results and Insights

Presenting your **analytical findings** effectively is one of the most crucial aspects of Business Analytics. The ultimate goal of any analytics project is to provide clear, actionable insights that can guide business decisions. How you present your findings can significantly impact how your audience understands, engages with, and acts upon your recommendations.

The presentation of business analytics should be structured, compelling, and tailored to the audience. Whether you're presenting to **executives**, **managers**, or **data scientists**, the communication approach should vary based on their familiarity with the subject and their decision-making needs.

Below, we will outline the **best practices** for showcasing your findings, along with strategies to make your presentation more effective.

1. Understand Your Audience

The first step in any presentation is to understand your **audience**:

- **Executives/Stakeholders**: These are often non-technical individuals interested in strategic insights and actionable recommendations.

- **Managers**: Managers may want more granular details that tie to operational decisions and team-level outcomes.

- **Technical Teams/Analysts**: Technical audiences may require deeper insights into the model-building process, methodology, and data.

Key considerations:

- **Executive Presentations**: Focus on the **big picture**, the **business impact**, and actionable recommendations.

- **Managerial Presentations**: Provide more detailed insights that help in decision-making and operational improvements.

- **Technical Presentations**: Dive into the methodology, metrics, and statistical significance of your analysis.

2. Start with the Business Problem

Before diving into numbers and models, **frame the problem** from a business perspective. This helps set the context and gives your audience a clear understanding of the **purpose** of the analysis.

- **Problem Definition**: Clearly state the business question you're answering. For example:
    - o "How can we reduce customer churn in the next quarter?"
    - o "What are the key drivers of sales growth in Region X?"

Example: If you're analyzing customer churn, begin by highlighting the impact of churn on revenue and the need for better retention strategies.

3. Visual Storytelling with Data

Visualization is one of the most powerful tools for presenting analytical results. Well-designed charts and graphs can help simplify complex information and make it more digestible for your audience. Use visualizations to tell a **story**, not just to display data.

Best Practices in Visualization:

- **Keep it Simple**: Use clear, intuitive charts. Avoid cluttered or overly complex visualizations.
- **Choose the Right Chart Type**: Different charts serve different purposes.
    - o **Bar/Column charts**: Great for comparing categories (e.g., sales by region).
    - o **Line charts**: Best for trends over time (e.g., sales performance month-over-month).
    - o **Pie charts**: Useful for showing proportions but should be used sparingly.
    - o **Heatmaps**: Excellent for correlation analysis or performance indicators.
    - o **Scatter plots**: Ideal for showing relationships between two variables.

Example:

- A **bar chart** showing the percentage of churned vs. retained customers in different segments.
- A **line graph** showing sales growth trends across regions over several months.

Tools for Visualization:

- **R** has powerful visualization libraries such as **ggplot2** and **plotly**, which can be used to create interactive and informative charts.

- **Power BI** or **Tableau** are business intelligence tools that are widely used for creating impactful dashboards and visualizations.

4. Focus on Key Insights and Actionable Recommendations

The goal of the analysis is not just to present numbers but to **translate** those numbers into actionable **insights**. Focus on what the data **reveals** and what it **means** for the business.

Key Insights:

- **Summary of findings**: Highlight the main takeaways from the analysis. For example:
    - "We found that customer churn increases significantly when service response time exceeds 48 hours."
    - "Marketing spend has a high positive correlation with sales growth in Region X."

Actionable Recommendations:

- Provide **concrete recommendations** based on the insights.
    - "To reduce churn, we should implement a 24-hour response time SLA."
    - "Increase marketing spend by 10% in Region X to further drive sales growth."

Recommendations should be **clear**, **specific**, and **feasible** based on the data.

5. Communicate Uncertainty and Limitations

Be transparent about the **uncertainties** in your analysis and the **limitations** of your models. This adds credibility to your work and sets realistic expectations.

- **Model limitations**: "The random forest model we used predicts churn with 85% accuracy, but there is still room for improvement."

- **Data limitations**: "Some data from our CRM system was missing, which could slightly impact the results."

6. Provide Context with Benchmarks or Historical Data

Providing **benchmarks** or **historical data** helps contextualize your findings and allows stakeholders to compare current performance against past trends or industry standards.

- **Example**: "Our sales growth of 5% this quarter is in line with the industry average of 4%, but slightly below our target of 7%."

7. Use Clear and Concise Language

Avoid jargon and overly technical terms, especially if your audience is not familiar with advanced analytics or statistics. Focus on **clarity** and **simplicity**.

- Instead of: "The p-value for the hypothesis test was 0.03, suggesting a statistically significant result."

- Say: "We found that the difference in sales between the two regions is statistically significant, with a 97% confidence level."

8. Tailor the Presentation to the Audience

Different stakeholders have different needs:

- **Executives**: Focus on high-level insights and business impact.

- **Managers**: Provide more detailed operational recommendations.

- **Technical Teams**: Dive into methodology, model performance, and data sources.

Example: If you're presenting to a marketing team, you might want to focus on insights around customer segments, marketing ROI, and engagement strategies. For a sales team, focus on lead generation, sales trends, and sales cycle insights.

9. Tell a Story with Your Data

Effective analytics presentations are not just about numbers—they're about telling a **story**. Use a narrative arc to guide the audience through your analysis:

1. **Set the Scene**: Start with the business problem or challenge.

2. **Present the Journey**: Walk through the data exploration, methodology, and analysis.

3. **Present the Conclusion**: Provide the key insights and actionable recommendations.

4. **Provide Next Steps**: What actions should the business take based on your analysis?

10. Practice and Refine Your Presentation

- **Rehearse** your presentation to ensure it flows smoothly and that you're able to answer questions confidently.

- **Seek Feedback**: Before presenting to stakeholders, practice with colleagues or mentors and get feedback.

- **Use Visual Aids**: Use slides or dashboards as a **visual aid**, but don't rely solely on them. You should be able to explain your insights without reading directly from your slides.

Example of a Structured Analytics Presentation

Slide 1: Title

- Title: "Customer Churn Prediction: Key Drivers and Actionable Insights"
- Your name, date, and company logo

Slide 2: Problem Statement

- **Business Problem**: "The company has seen an increase in churn, leading to a decline in revenue. We need to identify the key drivers of churn to take proactive measures."

Slide 3: Data Overview

- Briefly describe the dataset used (e.g., customer demographics, usage data, support interactions).
- "We analyzed data from 10,000 customers over the last 12 months."

Slide 4: Key Findings

- "Churn rates are highest among customers with low engagement and those who contacted customer support more than 3 times."
- "Price sensitivity is a major factor in churn for customers in the 25-35 age group."

Slide 5: Insights and Visuals

- Show charts of churn by customer segment (age, engagement, support calls).
- "Customers who have contacted support more than 3 times are 40% more likely to churn."

Slide 6: Recommendations

- "Introduce a loyalty program for high-engagement customers."
- "Provide additional support and personalized offers to customers with more than 3 support tickets."

Slide 7: Next Steps

- "Implement the loyalty program in the next quarter and track its impact on churn."

- "Investigate further into the reasons behind high support calls and implement a customer satisfaction survey."

Slide 8: Q&A

- Open the floor for questions and discussion.

Conclusion

The ability to present your analytical findings in a compelling way is as important as the analysis itself. By following these best practices, you can ensure that your insights resonate with your audience and lead to informed business decisions. Keep your presentations **clear**, **concise**, and **actionable**, and always tailor your message to the audience's level of expertise and business needs.

12.3 Future Directions in Business Analytics: Emerging Trends and Technologies

The field of **Business Analytics (BA)** is evolving rapidly, with new **technologies**, **techniques**, and **approaches** transforming how businesses leverage data for decision-making. In this section, we'll discuss the key **emerging trends** and **technologies** shaping the future of business analytics.

1. Artificial Intelligence (AI) and Machine Learning (ML) Integration

AI and **ML** are set to revolutionize business analytics by enhancing predictive capabilities, automating decision-making, and uncovering insights from complex datasets. While AI and ML have been part of the analytics landscape for years, their integration into everyday business processes is rapidly accelerating.

Key Developments:

- **Predictive Analytics**: Machine learning models can predict future trends with greater accuracy. For instance, **customer churn prediction**, **sales forecasting**, and **inventory optimization** are all applications powered by ML algorithms.

- **Natural Language Processing (NLP)**: NLP is enabling more intuitive interactions with data. Businesses can use conversational AI to analyze data, generate reports, and answer business questions directly from unstructured data sources like emails, chat logs, and social media.

- **Automated Decision Making**: AI-powered systems can make autonomous decisions based on data analysis, streamlining processes and improving efficiency in areas like marketing optimization and fraud detection.

Example:

- In retail, AI can be used to **forecast demand** based on historical trends, seasonality, and market conditions, which helps businesses optimize their supply chain and reduce excess inventory.

2. Augmented Analytics

Augmented Analytics refers to the use of AI, ML, and NLP to automate data preparation, data discovery, and insight generation. The goal is to make data analysis more accessible to non-technical users while improving the productivity of data scientists.

Key Developments:

- **Automated Data Preparation**: Augmented analytics tools help automate data cleaning, transformation, and integration tasks, which are typically time-consuming and require technical expertise.

- **Self-Service BI**: With augmented analytics, business users can generate reports, dashboards, and insights without needing advanced technical skills. AI-driven insights can also help uncover hidden patterns in the data.

- **Advanced Insights Discovery**: Tools now enable automatic identification of trends, anomalies, and patterns, reducing the need for manual hypothesis testing and exploratory analysis.

Example:

- A marketing team could use an augmented analytics platform to automatically generate customer segmentation reports, uncovering insights like high-value customers who may require a loyalty program without needing to rely on IT or data scientists for analysis.

3. Cloud Analytics

Cloud computing has already reshaped how businesses store and process data, but the future of cloud-based analytics is even more promising. Cloud analytics platforms are becoming more powerful, scalable, and cost-effective, enabling businesses to store vast amounts of data and run complex analyses without significant investment in on-premise infrastructure.

Key Developments:

- **Scalable Data Processing**: Cloud platforms like **AWS**, **Azure**, and **Google Cloud** offer on-demand compute resources, making it easier for businesses to scale their analytics as data volumes grow.

- **Cloud Data Lakes**: Instead of storing data in siloed databases, organizations are moving towards cloud-based **data lakes** to consolidate all types of structured and unstructured data. This enables easier access and analysis of large, diverse datasets.

- **Integration with Other Cloud Services**: Cloud analytics tools now integrate seamlessly with other cloud services, such as machine learning tools, CRM platforms, and business intelligence applications.

Example:

- A large e-commerce company may use cloud analytics to collect and process real-time transaction data, customer browsing behavior, and inventory levels across various platforms, using that data for real-time decision-making.

4. Edge Analytics and IoT

With the explosion of Internet of Things (**IoT**) devices and the increase in real-time data generation, **edge analytics** has emerged as a key trend. Instead of sending all raw data to the cloud for processing, edge analytics involves processing data at or near the source (on the device or local server), enabling faster insights and more efficient decision-making.

Key Developments:

- **Real-Time Data Processing**: For industries such as manufacturing, transportation, and healthcare, edge analytics enables the real-time monitoring of equipment, machinery, and patient health. This reduces latency and allows businesses to act on insights quickly.

- **Autonomous Systems**: In IoT-driven environments, edge analytics can be used to optimize processes without human intervention, such as monitoring factory machines and automatically adjusting operations based on real-time performance data.

Example:

- In **smart cities**, IoT sensors and edge computing can collect data on traffic, air quality, and energy consumption. This data is processed locally to optimize traffic flow or detect potential hazards before sending summaries to the central system for further analysis.

5. Data Privacy and Governance

As data privacy concerns grow, **data governance** and **privacy protection** will continue to be a major focus for businesses. The rise of **GDPR (General Data Protection Regulation)** and similar regulations worldwide will drive the need for businesses to implement stronger data governance frameworks.

Key Developments:

- **Data Sovereignty**: The demand for local data storage and processing is increasing to comply with regional data protection regulations.

- **Data Anonymization**: Businesses are focusing on developing techniques for **anonymizing** or **pseudonymizing** sensitive customer data to ensure compliance with privacy laws.

- **Governance Automation**: Automation tools will be used to enforce policies and monitor data usage across the organization, ensuring that data is used ethically and in compliance with regulations.

Example:

- A healthcare provider that uses patient data for analysis would need to ensure that all data is anonymized or securely encrypted to comply with **HIPAA** (Health Insurance Portability and Accountability Act) regulations in the U.S.

6. Explainable AI (XAI)

As businesses increasingly rely on **AI** and **ML** models for decision-making, **explainability** of these models is becoming more critical. **Explainable AI (XAI)** focuses on creating machine learning models that can provide **clear and understandable explanations** for their predictions, making them more transparent and trustworthy.

Key Developments:

- **Model Interpretability**: Tools are being developed to allow users to interpret the outcomes of black-box models (like deep learning and random forests) by identifying which features contributed to predictions.

- **Regulatory Compliance**: Many sectors, such as finance and healthcare, require transparency and accountability in AI-driven decision-making, making **XAI** an essential development.

Example:

- A **loan approval** system powered by AI could use explainable AI to show why an application was approved or denied, such as "The applicant's credit score was a major factor, and the employment history was a key consideration."

7. Automated Machine Learning (AutoML)

AutoML is making machine learning more accessible to non-technical users by automating the process of model selection, training, and evaluation. Rather than requiring extensive knowledge of algorithms and hyperparameters, **AutoML platforms** allow business users and analysts to apply machine learning models to their data with minimal effort.

Key Developments:

- **End-to-End Automation**: AutoML tools can handle the entire machine learning pipeline—from data preprocessing to model deployment—without requiring human intervention.

- **Lowering Barriers**: By automating much of the machine learning workflow, AutoML makes it easier for businesses of all sizes to apply machine learning without needing specialized expertise.

Example:

- A retail business could use **AutoML** tools to predict customer purchase behavior by uploading historical sales data, and the system would automatically select and tune the best machine learning model for prediction.

8. Blockchain in Data Analytics

Blockchain technology, best known for its role in cryptocurrency, is emerging as a tool for enhancing **data security** and **transparency** in analytics. Blockchain's decentralized nature ensures that data is immutable and verifiable, making it particularly useful in industries that rely heavily on data integrity.

Key Developments:

- **Data Provenance**: Blockchain can be used to track the origin of data and ensure its integrity, which is crucial in industries like finance, healthcare, and supply chain.

- **Smart Contracts**: In data analytics, blockchain-based smart contracts could automate data sharing between organizations and ensure that data is used in accordance with agreed-upon rules.

Example:

- A **supply chain** company could use blockchain to track the provenance of raw materials from farm to factory, ensuring the data's accuracy and transparency while protecting the privacy of suppliers.

9. Real-Time Analytics

Real-time or **streaming analytics** allows businesses to analyze and act on data as it is generated. This is critical in industries where time-sensitive decisions are crucial, such as in **financial trading**, **online advertising**, and **IoT applications**.

Key Developments:

- **Real-Time Decision Making**: Businesses can instantly detect trends, anomalies, or opportunities and take immediate action. For example, fraud detection systems in banking can flag suspicious transactions in real-time.

- **Integration with IoT**: Real-time analytics allows businesses to monitor IoT devices and sensors continuously, making it possible to optimize operations instantly.

Example:

- An **e-commerce platform** could use real-time analytics to recommend products to users as they browse, adjusting in real-time based on user behavior and preferences.

Conclusion

The future of **Business Analytics** is marked by an increasing integration of **advanced technologies** such as AI, machine learning, cloud computing, and edge analytics. As businesses continue to adopt and harness these technologies, they will gain deeper, more actionable insights that can drive **operational efficiency, enhanced customer experiences**, and **innovative business strategies**.

Key trends to watch out for in the future of business analytics include **augmented analytics, automated machine learning, real-time analytics**, and **blockchain**, all of which will shape the ways companies make data-driven decisions. Staying ahead of these trends and embracing emerging technologies will be critical for businesses aiming to stay competitive in the data-driven world of tomorrow.